The Customer Satisfaction Audit

An Eight Step Approach to Ensure That Your Firm Stays Focused on Customer Needs to Promote Real Gains

Abram I. Bluestein, Michael Moriarty & Ronald J. Sanderson

A.T. Kearney, Inc.

CSP

Cambridge Strategy Publications Ltd.
Station Offices
Station Yard
Axminster
Devon. EX13 5PF
United Kingdom

www.cambridgestrategy.com

Contents

Second Edition: 2008

ISBN 978-1-902433-98-1

Part 1

The Customer Satisfaction Audit

This audit is structured in three parts. Part 1 examines the process of carrying out a customer satisfaction audit. Part 2 looks at the audit process itself and provides a framework that addresses some of the logistical and process requirements of conducting an audit. Part 3 comprises a series of questions based on the eight steps in Part 1. These questions are designed to help you plan and implement your audit in a straightforward and practical manner.

While individual examples are taken from named service or (more often) manufacturing sectors, all of them can be adapted to your own business. Indeed, for many years, benchmarking has shown the value to be gained by a company comparing its core practices with those of companies in quite different sectors: airports learnt from sports stadiums about handling high volumes of impatient customers, while inventory management in a hotel chain has much in common with that in a vehicle manufacturing plant.

INTRODUCTION

The adage "Service with a smile" implies that customer service is a novelty that is tacked on to a company's core business. This view of service oversimplifies the importance of meeting the needs of customers. Customer service involves much more than the delivery of a product or service to the customer.

In the same way, achieving customer satisfaction requires satisfying all of the customer's requirements. Customers are the ultimate judge of what those requirements are, and what level of service and quality is acceptable. They judge their satisfaction not only by the product itself, but also by the totality of the experience that comes with it. Satisfied customers feel that they have experienced the right combination of product quality, marketing and sales support, price, reputation, product design, and ease of doing business. They also consider on-time, complete and reliable "customer service." Total customer satisfaction is achieved by providing a product and service portfolio that exceeds all of the customer's expectations.

Although the media is filled with articles about customer satisfaction, few companies have made the strategic and operational changes required to completely satisfy customers, even though the benefits of doing so can be great. It is becoming more apparent that the only sustainable competitive advantage in the future will be one that is based on satisfying customers thoroughly.

Companies that succeed in satisfying their customers do not have to match their competitors' low prices. Their customers are loyal because the value offered by the product or service is high. These companies also improve asset and expense productivity by eliminating operations that do not add to customer value. Companies that have high levels of customer satisfaction also achieve incremental market share penetration over their competitors and realize faster growth in market capitalization (share price).

The total customer satisfaction process is new to most companies. Research on customer satisfaction demonstrates that less than one-third of all companies have a well-developed and coherent customer satisfaction process that is linked to operating strategies and plans. However, many companies do have elements of a total customer satisfaction process in place — survey techniques, sales force feedback activities, market segmentation strategies or innovative order entry and fulfillment techniques.

This audit deals with making total customer satisfaction the basis for achieving competitive advantage. Achieving this complex objective requires organization-wide commitment to meeting customer demands. Sometimes it calls for radical changes in the way a company thinks about its way of doing business. Using customer satisfaction as a criterion for decision making means basing choices on subjective judgments and information (customer perceptions of the company's performance and competitors' performance) and not objective, measurable inputs (number of phone calls taken, quantity of orders filled) that may have been used in the past.

This self-assessment will create a deeper awareness of what is necessary to succeed in today's customer satisfaction environment. It provides a mechanism for auditing the existing customer satisfaction process in a company and describes the process of developing a total customer satisfaction strategy. It also provides examples to raise awareness of the critical importance of total customer satisfaction to overall competitiveness. Finally, this assessment will outline opportunities to create tangible results.

WHAT TO EXPECT FROM A CUSTOMER SATISFACTION AUDIT

The future of customer satisfaction is a logical extension of its past. After World War II, pent-up demand put a premium on production. Those manufacturers that had productive capacity could push their products into the market and be assured that they would be valued. Companies that could produce at a lower cost had a competitive advantage over others in their industry. As overall productive capacity increased, the priorities of customers changed from whether to buy a particular product to which kind of product to buy from a growing range of products. Customers began placing demands on manufacturers that were met largely through improvements in physical distribution infrastructures and more effective marketing. The 1960s were the decade of "new and improved" extensions of everything -even branded produce such as bananas and tomatoes was marketed effectively. This was made possible by innovations in logistics.

However, in the 1970s and 1980s, two important changes influenced forever the way customers and suppliers dealt with each other. First, world energy price fluctuations and the unfixing of foreign exchange rate agreements resulted in an economic upheaval which led to disorder in the global marketplace. This caused the beginning of the shift away from customer focus on "price" to customer focus on "total cost," or the total of all of the costs of buying and using a product or service. This shift continues today. For example, soaring interest rates in the US in the 19705 made retailers highly sensitive to inventory holding costs. This spurred an industry-wide shift away from "back room" inventory storage to just-in-time, direct delivery to grocery stores on a daily basis. Second, an information revolution was born that has allowed customers and suppliers alike to more effectively measure and manage the elements of that "total cost." Databanks that would have filled a large room in 1967 now fit in the hand-held terminal used to manage and maintain shelf inventories and order quantities. This has led to a complete reversal in the way purchase decisions are driven. Fifty years ago, most customer decisions were "pushed" by a manufacturer's capability to produce, as illustrated in Figure 1.

FIGURE 1
MANUFACTURING 'PUSH' SUPPLY CHAIN

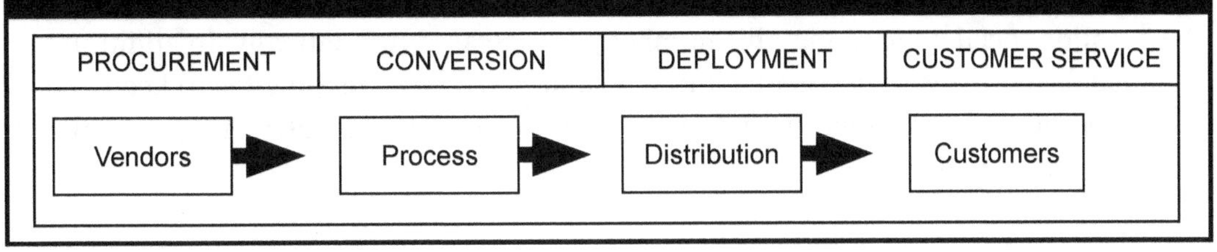

Now, most production decisions are "pulled" by the customer's desire to consume, as illustrated in Figure 2. The resulting challenge for business leaders in the 21st century will be to transform their strategies from focusing on competing in a particular link in this chain — as supplier, manufacturer, or distributor — to focusing on competing as a partner with others in the chain with total customer satisfaction as the end goal. This is equally true of the service sector and everywhere requires increased integration between functions within a company, as well as collaboration between companies.

FIGURE 2
CUSTOMER 'PULL' SUPPLY CHAIN

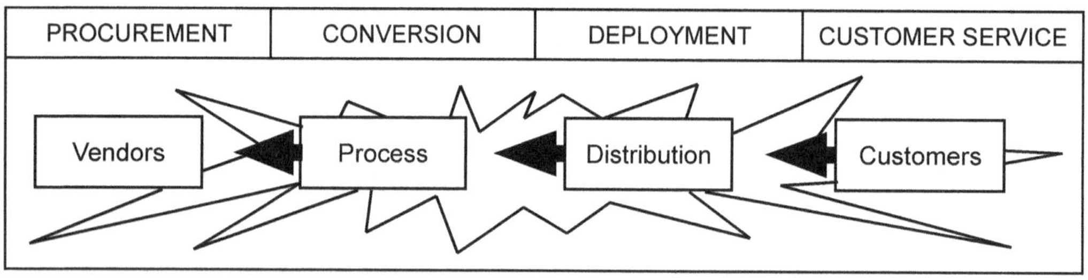

Supply Chain Partners and Total Satisfaction

This concept of a "supply chain" has become widely used to describe and define the linkages and relationships among each of the supply chain partners. More important, the concept of the supply chain suggests that the focus of each "link" in the chain must be on end-user customer value and satisfaction. This means that companies who serve the same end users are learning to cooperate in order to maximize that customer's satisfaction as the end link. Satisfied customers are clearly the most important part of a supply chain because they pay the money that supports all other activity in the chain. Therefore, the other partners in the chain should be unified by the goal of satisfying the end link. It is useless to save money making a product or service that customers do not value.

The importance of satisfied customers is nevertheless often overlooked. The old wisdom was that delighted and dissatisfied customers would tell an average of five other people about their experience with a product or service. This was true for both industrial markets and consumer markets. With the advent of sophisticated consumer protection and shopping comparison websites and the remorseless growth of online social networking, this number has increased dramatically. In addition, it usually costs five times as much to woo and win a new customer as to keep one totally satisfied. All other things being equal, the return on investment from satisfying customers is remarkable.

A *Fortune* magazine and Forum Corporation study detailed the following competitive risks of not totally satisfying customers:

- Since service, quality and total satisfaction are increasingly important variables in every customer's value equation, 68 percent of customers who are disappointed enough to leave their suppliers do so because of poor service, rather than because of price or product quality problems.

- Ninety-eight percent of dissatisfied customers never complain to the company they are disappointed with.

- Most unhappy customers abandon supply chains, not individual companies. Increasingly, sophisticated customers recognize that a company's competitiveness rises and falls with that of its supply chain partners. For example, auto manufacturers in North America realized that sales were being lost due to the failure of their dealer networks to satisfy customers. As a result, they have taken steps to work around their dealers with fixed "value pricing" and other methods. The one bad link in the chain was hurting business for all the supply chain's partners.

The good news of the supply chain concept is that dissatisfied customers may seek out another supply chain in which a particular company participates. The bad news is that companies may alienate and lose customers for actions (or a lack of action) over which they have little direct control.

Many companies can make a profit because of a technological innovation, or a timely market entry, or a structural barrier to competition. However, these profits will evaporate over time as technology matures, time passes, and barriers are broken down. The number of products that were initially developed by North Americans but successfully merchandised by Asians shows that innovation alone cannot satisfy customers. The only sustainable competitive advantage is one that is based on totally satisfying customers. Achieving that advantage must be an objective shared by all members of the supply chain.

THE TOTAL CUSTOMER SATISFACTION PROCESS

Many companies are still organized by largely independent functions, each of which is driven by largely unrelated (and often contradictory) goals. The sales force moves toward the goal of increasing volume, while the manufacturing or service delivery function attempts to reduce costs. R&D invests in the development of new products, while finance tries to maximize current financial position. Adopting a total customer satisfaction approach to doing business means that the goal of meeting customer demands cuts across all of these traditional boundaries. When this happens, traditional functional goals are no longer relevant, and determining which factors lead to success for each function will usually be less clear-cut, as shown in Figure 3. Thus, the system becomes more effective, but also more complex.

FIGURE 3
TRADITIONAL VERSUS CUSTOMER-CENTRED MEASURES

	TRADITIONAL	CUSTOMER-CENTERED
UNIT COSTS	• Lowest unit cost	• Balanced with customer requirements to achieve lowest system cost
INVENTORIES	• Continuous reduction	• Matched to service needs
DISTRIBUTION	• Reduced transportation and manufacturing costs	• Service-adjusted costs
FILL RATES	• Maximize	• Measured against promises

Figure 4 shows the process for creating a cycle of customer satisfaction. The total customer satisfaction process requires strategic investments coupled with organizational restructuring. Investing strategically means committing resources to those areas that will increase an organization's ability to meet the needs of its customers, rather than subordinating this need to cost reduction priorities. Some of these areas might include employee recruitment and training, or providing follow-up service. Organizational restructuring is necessary when

FIGURE 4
THE CYCLE OF SATISFACTION

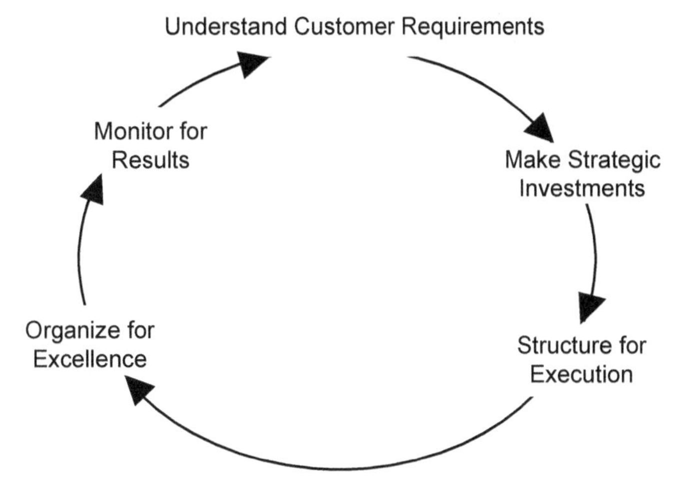

traditional barriers isolate functions and discourage them from working together to meet customer demands. This means that traditional functional goals must be abandoned and replaced by cross-functional objectives. Ultimate competitive success depends on getting feedback from customers and launching the process anew.

Many managers fail to understand what keeps their companies from performing like customer satisfaction leaders Caterpillar, Inc., Cable News Network, Nissan Motors Co., Singapore Airlines and Federal Express. The leaders of these companies have learned that they must listen to customers and respond to what customers say they want. Nissan set a new standard for engineering-driven automobile manufacturers by putting new model form-fit-function design into the hands of customer teams. Federal Express counts its service failures not in percentages like most companies, but in absolute numbers: every single service failure is a lost opportunity to delight a customer. Leaders like these exhibit characteristics that demonstrate the difference made by customer-focused management.

WHY COMPANIES DON'T SATISFY THEIR CUSTOMERS

Although this process seems quite simple and straightforward, many companies fail to make it a routine part of their management systems. There are four reasons why companies fail to incorporate what they know about customer requirements into the organization's overall strategy:

- They don't understand customer needs.
- They don't understand their own performance.
- They lack commitment to customer satisfaction.
- They haven't overcome the myths that obstruct action.

A review of each of these obstacles will show how they influence a company's ability to build a strategy based on satisfying customers.

Companies Don't Understand Customer Needs

According to the research reflected in Figure 5, there are significant differences in the way customers perceive their needs as compared to how suppliers see those same requirements.

FIGURE 5
MATCH BETWEEN CUSTOMER'S ACTUAL REQUIREMENTS AND SUPPLIER'S PERCEPTION

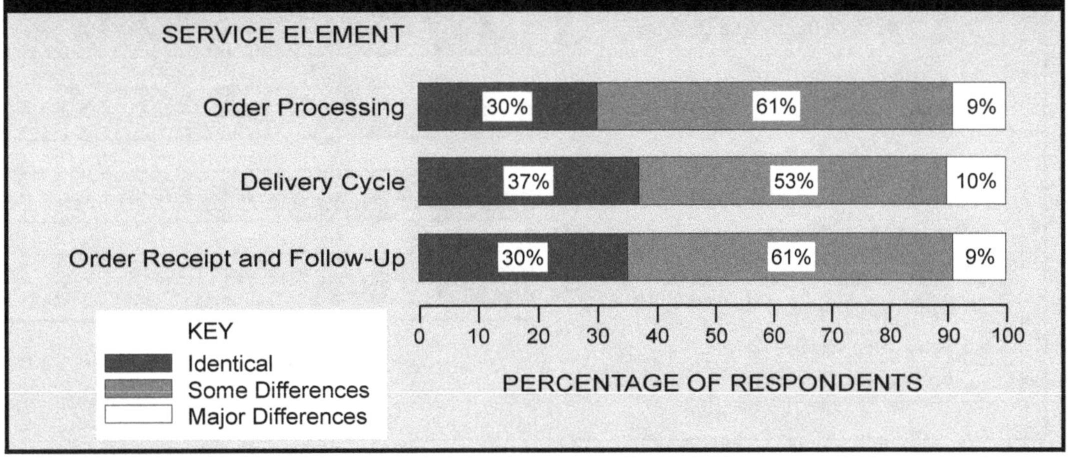

Most suppliers misunderstand customer needs along at least three important dimensions: order processing, delivery cycle, and order receipt and follow-up. In other research to determine how accurately customers thought suppliers understood their needs, two-thirds of customers said they believed their needs were either seriously or somewhat misunderstood by their suppliers. Further research showed most suppliers perceived frequent contact with customers to be far less important than their customers did in identifying customer requirements. Over a quarter of the companies studied did not systematically update their understanding of customer needs, or did so only once every two or three years.

Companies Don't Understand Their Own Performance

Even when companies have determined what their customers want, they frequently fail to monitor their performance against those targets. More importantly, they do not understand their customers' perceptions of their performance against those targets. Figure 6 shows how suppliers' perception of their ability to fulfill customer needs is generally much higher than the corresponding perceptions of their customers.

Even if a company understands what customers require to be totally satisfied, and understands how its current performance stacks up against those requirements, it may

FIGURE 6
CUSTOMER VERSUS SUPPLIER VIEWS ON MEETING QUANTITATIVE GOALS

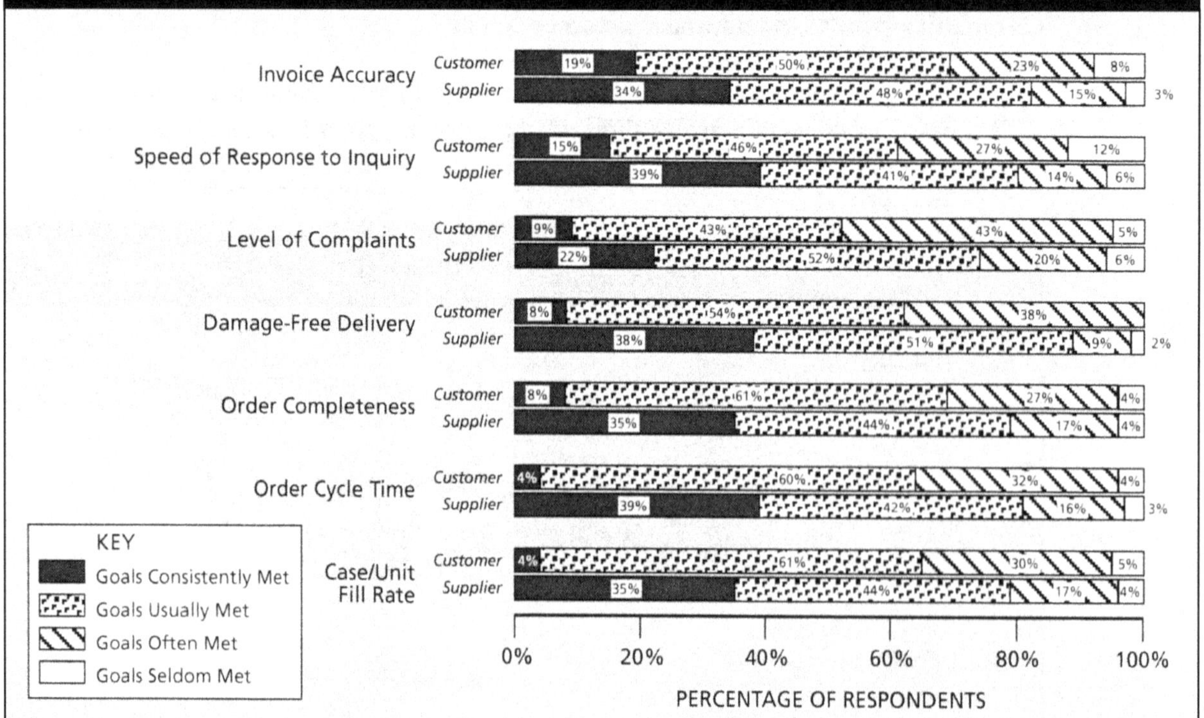

lack the commitment to achieve those targets (and to create the perception in the minds of its customers that it is achieving those targets). Organizational issues of structure, skill availability, culture, and management process often get in the way of total customer satisfaction, the element that actually results in increased sales. While these companies may be successful in the short term, their long-term competitiveness is compromised by failing to win customer loyalty.

Management Lacks Commitment to Customer Satisfaction

How can an observer tell when management lacks commitment to satisfying its customers? Here are a few diagnostic questions:

- Are decisions made that adversely affect customer satisfaction, and then justified because they will improve short-term financial position?
- Are disagreements between production or front-line service and sales allowed to continue on for months before a compromise is reached? Do compromises focus on totally satisfying customers?
- Does the senior operating executive get personally involved in understanding customer satisfaction performance? Is executive and functional manager compensation related to success at satisfying customers?
- Are monthly management information packages based on strictly financial figures, or are operating performance measures included?

Competitive advantage based on customer satisfaction cuts across traditional functional boundaries, and top executives and functional managers must be its most ardent supporters.

Organizations Are Victims of Customer Satisfaction Myths

Finally, many companies are still plagued by myths that keep them from achieving total customer satisfaction. These myths build up over time as a result of company tradition, parochialism, management shortsightedness, or misinformation. Auditors should review the following list to determine whether or not an organization is limited by a belief in customer satisfaction myths:

- *Price is the only thing that matters.* This is becoming less and less true as customers look at the total cost of a product or service rather than merely its sales price. Even companies whose commodity-type products compete primarily on price now provide value-adding services in order to distinguish their products.

- *We're already at 99 percent.* In today's competitive environment, 99 percent isn't good enough. Few customers would put up with electric service that was unavailable for 14 minutes every day, or drinking water that was unpotable four days each year. Most people would tire of a book with five typographical errors on each page. Why should corporate leaders think their own customers are any less demanding? Ninety-nine percent performance begs to be beaten by competitors.

- *Our customer service department handles that.* There are usually dozens of contact points between a company and its customers. A company's accounts department may have more frequent contact with its customers than its sales department. Most customers see more of a supplier's invoices than of its promotion materials. Everyone in an organization is responsible for satisfying its customers, and it is a key business activity in which people in every function must participate.

- *We understand their needs / Customers won't involve us / We can't afford to give customers what they want.* By now the fallacy of these statements is plain. Customer needs change constantly, so managers should never feel complacent about understanding their requirements. Customers are eager to share their needs, and companies that ignore the customer's voice will not survive in the long term.

Requirements of an Effective Customer Service Program

These characteristics are common among companies that have established a record of satisfying customers:

- *Letting customers define service value*

Too often, management sets service levels according to its own standards. This standard is rarely defined by the customer's perception of value, or measured in terms of customer satisfaction. Many companies measure their fill rates against orders entered, and cycle times from the time an order is entered until it is shipped. More effective measures would gauge differences between the order that was entered and what the customer really wanted to order, or order cycle time before order entry. Because these factors are much more difficult to measure, few companies make any effort to understand the totality of their customers' ordering experience. This experience extends from the customer's perception of the company's image to the level of assurance of satisfaction. It ranges from total value perception and security to disaster recovery capability. An effective customer satisfaction program examines the needs of the customer along all of these dimensions.

The success of the convenience store industry demonstrates the competitive power of matching customer preferences with product and service delivery capability. An analysis of product value measured only in terms of price would predict the failure of these high priced, conveniently located stores that carry a limited inventory. Yet customers value the convenience provided by this channel enough to allow it to compete with vigor and profitability against supermarkets and discount stores.

- *Exceeding customers' expectations in key areas, not all areas*

Achieving competitive advantage through total customer satisfaction does *not* mean being "all things to all people" or excelling in every customer service category. It means providing quality service in all areas, and exceptional quality in areas that customers value the most. McDonalds' customers don't expect *Guide Bleu* ambiance; they expect consistently prepared food at reasonable prices without waiting.

Exceeding customer satisfaction expectations in key areas rarely requires superhuman effort or monumental investments. It does require that decision makers listen to customers and respond to their needs. For example, First National Bank of Chicago segmented the lobby in its flagship bank so that customers with brief, routine transactions are not required to wait in long lines behind people whose needs require more of a teller's time.

- *Differentiating the customer base and investing to serve profitable customers*

Many companies in the apparel manufacturing and retailing industries are differentiated according to specific customers. For example, some focus on the needs of the big and tall market, while others cater to various lifestyle groups. This strategy works because customers will pay more to have their needs met more precisely. Companies in other industries serve a more varied clientele but prioritize their efforts according to other criteria. Federal Express developed an entirely new market based on the fact that many customers wanted faster mail delivery, and would be willing to pay premium prices for it. The principle of a customer satisfaction-focused strategy is the same: tailor a service identity to the high-profit customer within your target segment.

- *Investing in training, education and systems*

Customers may define what quality service is, but the employees of a company are ultimately responsible for delivering that service. Employee hiring, training and education are key strategic investments for customer satisfaction leaders like General Electric (GE), American Airlines and The Four Seasons Hotel chain. GE's hiring process includes an extensive candidate identification and selection program, which involves the profiling and interviewing of prospective employees. Once a candidate has been hired, an intensive, ongoing training program teaches newcomers to the organization about the needs of that company's customers. For example, the GE answer center in Kentucky responds to 3,000,000 calls every year and resolves 90 percent of customer inquiries on the first call. Although such programs are costly, they make significant contributions to the achievement of the company's strategy. American Airlines, another company that relies heavily on the ability of its front-line employees to meet customer needs, invested hundreds of millions of dollars in a training center which accommodates 800 people at a time.

Employees must also have access to the authority, information, and resources to provide service. Two of the world's best known service leaders, American Express and Federal Express, literally put those tools in employees' hands. American Express uses Authorizer's Assistant, an artificial intelligence-based decision support software, to assist representatives in approving cardholders' purchases quickly and efficiently. Federal Express revolutionized the business with its early introduction of hand-held package monitors to access information about a customer's delivery.

Make Outstanding Customer Service a Primary Goal

Top corporations throughout the world consistently outshine their less-effective competitors along the following dimensions:

- Systematically hear and respond to customers.

- Communicate a clear vision of what satisfaction means throughout the company.
- Establish measurable standards of service quality.
- Measure the company's performance against those standards continuously.

As customers become increasingly sophisticated, they are more likely to measure the service performance of those they buy from. Industrial customers are especially conscious of the bottom-line value of higher service levels. Savvy industrial buyers are implementing supplier service measurement systems that go far beyond tracking on-time delivery. Using an activity-based approach, service failures are monitored and weighted according to their impact on the customer's own business processes.

For example, a missing part may get a weighting of 1, while a defective part that causes downtime on a production line may get a weighting of 75. Suppliers are monitored over time, and the results of these measures go into the periodic reevaluation of supply sources. When more than one supplier provides a product or service, companies who monitor the service quality of their suppliers can make a buying decision or re-negotiate prices using historic failure costs to more accurately determine the true total cost of what they are buying.

As products mature, service quality increases in importance in proportion to other elements of the competitive portfolio. A study in the engineered components and subsystems industry asked the question, "What makes a supplier ideal?" in the eyes of key customers. Results of the research showed that the *how* of the product/service portfolio is almost twice as important as the *what*. Details of the study are shown in Figure 7.

Product quality and technology are now often only the entry ticket to the competitive game. Remaining competitive depends on maintaining good customer relationships. Customer satisfaction can even define the business, creating new industries and niches, as illustrated by the following examples:

- For years, the chemical distribution industry in North America grew at a more rapid rate than the chemical manufacturing industry did. This feat was accomplished

FIGURE 7
'HOW' IS MORE IMPORTANT THAN 'WHAT'

ENGINEERED COMPONENTS AND SUBSYSTEMS	
PRODUCT	
• Quality and reliability	20.3%
• Technology	10.6%
SUBTOTAL	**30.9%**
SERVICE	
• Delivery and timing	10.1%
• Responsiveness	55.2%
SUBTOTAL	**65.3%**
VALUE	**3.8%**
TOTAL	**100%**

by focusing on the customers' need for flexibility in packaging and delivery. Chemical manufacturers couldn't respond effectively to customer demands, and so lost valuable sales to value-added redistributors who could.

- Joseph T. Ryerson & Son became a triumphant competitor by recognizing that customers purchase what steel can be made into, not steel itself. Ryerson developed steel service centers that help customers select metals and alloys and provide post-production services like cutting, punching, bending and milling.

Other Benefits of Effective Customer Satisfaction Programs

Total customer satisfaction is the only externally-oriented goal that can unite a complete organization for market success and production efficiencies. Focusing on the customer avoids one of the most destructive traditions in business: the erection of fences between functions such as production, marketing and distribution. Even more significant, customer requirements are the only demands that manufacturers, service providers, wholesalers, retailers and commodity suppliers have in common. Accordingly, a focus on customer satisfaction can unify the entire supply chain.

The bottom line presents the most important reason to strive for total customer satisfaction. The Strategic Planning Institute of Cambridge, Massachusetts analyzed the performance of 2,600 businesses over 15 years and determined that financial performance is tied to the perceived quality of a company's goods and services. Companies whose quality/service portfolio ranked in the top third of their industry out earned their competitors by a two-to-one margin. Service quality commands a premium market price: according to the same study, companies in the upper half of service quality realized an average price nine percent higher than those of their competitors.

The value and importance of customer satisfaction make it essential that every company have an orderly process for satisfying its customers. Even more important, leading companies continually test the effectiveness of their approach to total customer satisfaction. The following sections describe one commonly used approach for doing this.

The next section provides a framework for thinking about a company's evolution in terms of customer satisfaction. Then guidelines are presented for auditing customer satisfaction performance.

USING THE STAGES OF EXCELLENCE FRAMEWORK

Much of what a company can do to improve its customer satisfaction performance depends on its stage of maturity. A.T. Kearney has developed a framework that describes a company's Stages of Excellence. It explains how companies change in a predictable pattern of growth. This framework is described briefly below, with additional information about how the model applies specifically to the improvement of customer satisfaction. This framework can help an audit team to understand its company's maturity in terms of satisfying customers. Once a company's maturity has been assessed, the framework also leads to conclusions about what type of intervention is appropriate.

Characteristics of the Stages of Excellence

Figure 8 shows the qualitative description of attributes of each stage for a customer satisfaction process.

FIGURE 8
CHARACTERISTICS OF STAGES OF EXCELLENCE

	STAGE I	STAGE II	STAGE III
CUSTOMER FOCUS	• Focus on each transaction	• Focus on market segment level requirements	• Provide differentiated service for individual customers
SCOPE/DEFINITION	• Product performance and price factors only	• Includes basic service levels: fill rates, delivery times, order cycle time	• Includes 'value-added' factors, e.g. working relationships, flexibility, communications
GOALS	• Minimize problems	• Achieve internally set goals	• Meet/exceed customer expectations
DETERMINING REQUIREMENTS	• Based on internal management opinion	• Salesforce opinions • Customer complaints	• Individual customer requirements/ expectations
SERVICE STRATEGY	• React to problems as they occur	• Minimize costs through efficient service	• Provide 'value-added' through partnerships and focus on total supply chain
PERFORMANCE MEASUREMENTS	• Sales volume	• Basic service levels: fill rates, delivery times	• Total customer satisfaction, including product, economic, marketing/sales, service and corporate factors
PERFORMANCE MEASURING APPROACH	• None	• Periodic tracking of service levels	• Ongoing monitoring of total satisfaction
MANAGEMENT PROCESS	• None	• Customer service department managers	• Culture of customer satisfaction throughout organization

Stage I companies are entrepreneurial in nature and have few policies and procedures. Key decisions are often made by one individual. Management processes are informal and work well when the organization is small and closely knit; they tend to break down when a company or business unit becomes too large to be managed by a single person.

Customer satisfaction performance in Stage I is characterized by "clearing the inbox" and responding to "forest fires" as they begin to burn out of control. The customer satisfaction strategy is strictly responsive. In general, Stage I companies do not rely on superior customer satisfaction to achieve or maintain competitive advantage. Unless market position is protected by patent or policy, Stage I companies rapidly develop budgets and cost controls in order to manage the customer service function more efficiently.

A company begins to move from Stage I to Stage II when management begins to adopt financial and other basic management controls and procedures. This often involves identifying opportunities and developing an action plan for improvement. When implemented, the focus is usually on cost reduction.

Stage II companies have tight financial controls structured around a comprehensive budgeting and control process. Making the budget is the number one objective. Internal management meetings are scheduled to coincide with budget reporting periods and financial results are usually the first item on the agenda. Stage II companies often become bureaucratic and focus internally on budget results rather than externally on customers or competitors. Most major corporations today function largely in Stage II.

Stage II customer satisfaction performance is characterized by the functional approach to customer satisfaction. The customer service department has a cost budget and is charged with executing a service strategy that emphasizes efficiency and minimizing unit cost to serve. Service levels are tracked, but they are usually compared with internally-focused goals that may have little relevance to true customer requirements. As products and markets mature, Stage II companies need to distinguish themselves on the basis of service in order to compete against niche product/service players. Increasingly, Stage II companies will find they are over-serving some classes of customers while under-serving others.

A company begins moving from Stage II to Stage III when it begins to look outward to learn what competitors are doing, what customers want, and what constitutes competitive performance. They begin to pursue functional excellence in one or more parts of the business. Management asks benchmarking questions such as, "What services do my customers really need? Are my costs as low as those of my competitors?"

Stage III companies have achieved excellence in one or more business areas. In those areas, they use non-financial performance measures to drive management decisions rather than relying on budget performance. Most Stage III companies have planning horizons of a year or more, with formal management objectives focused on improving performance over time rather than just managing current performance. Various service offerings are likely to be differentiated by type or class of customer, product, or other criteria to match cost with value from the customer's perspective.

Companies with Stage III customer satisfaction processes have an awareness of total customer satisfaction as the foundation of a competitive strategy. They strive to understand and respond to customer needs. Their strategies are energized by a commitment to meeting and exceeding customer expectations. The culture and management processes of Stage III companies supports the total customer satisfaction focus throughout the organization.

The Kearney model also specifies the dimensions for achieving Stage IV. These companies blur the traditional functional organization structures found in other stages and refocus their management around key business processes. For example, these companies may form multifunctional teams focused on the common goal of satisfying the ultimate customer or on new product development. Regardless of how advanced many leading companies are today, few actually operate as Stage IV companies. This is because their suppliers and customers still operate in Stages I, II or III, limiting the company's ability to fully develop Stage IV characteristics.

Because most of the companies who are engaged in the audit process are likely functioning in Stage II or Stage III, this assessment guide will emphasize making the transition between these stages and maximizing performance in Stage III. Stage III is where companies should be if they hope to establish a competitive advantage based on customer satisfaction. Later in this assessment, characteristics of customer satisfaction performance at each stage will be provided. This will enable audit teams to measure the performance of their customer satisfaction processes against the Stages of Excellence model.

The rest of this self-assessment is designed to help an audit team determine what its company's current customer strategy is, and to identify what changes need to be made in that strategy in order to achieve excellence in customer satisfaction.

STEPS IN CONDUCTING A CUSTOMER SATISFACTION AUDIT

The following steps provide information that will enable managers to measure a company's performance in understanding and meeting customer requirements.

Step 1: Understand Customer Requirements

Step 2: Analyze Current Capabilities

Step 3: Assess Competitors' Capabilities

Step 4: Identify Gaps

Step 5: Identify Options to Gain Strategic Service Advantage

Step 6: Analyze Trade-Offs

Step 7: Select Service Dimensions to Compete On

Step 8: Structure Service Offerings and Set Goals

This process of transforming raw customer requirements into a coherent customer satisfaction strategy is depicted graphically in Figure 9. This eight-step process is

FIGURE 9
FRAMEWORK FOR DEVELOPING A SERVICE STRATEGY

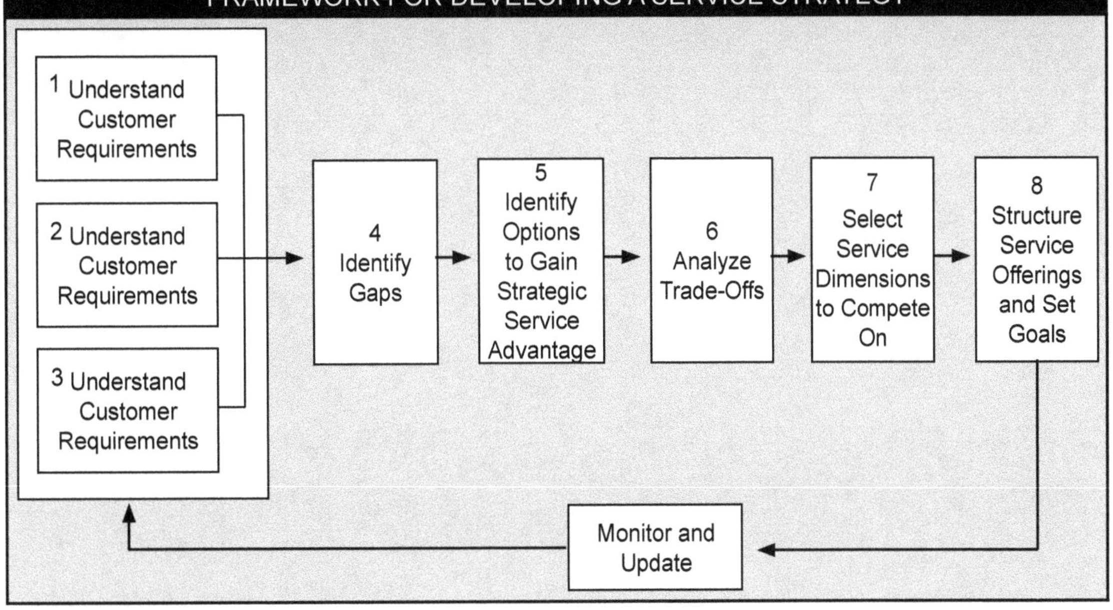

repeated continuously as customer requirements — and the company's ability to meet and exceed them — change and evolve. These steps will be discussed in greater detail.

Who Should Conduct the Audit?

The most effective tool for auditing a company's performance in terms of customer satisfaction is a cross-functional team of talented people that has the strong support of top management. A customer satisfaction strategy is not laid on top of a marketing strategy or a manufacturing strategy; it is a combination of these strategies. Team members should be chosen carefully; they should be the people who are expected to lead the company in the next decade. In a company, auditing the processes that contribute to customer satisfaction implies a commitment to improve those processes. Making these improvements requires a great deal of energy and dedication. If no such commitment exists, then the audit will be a wasted effort.

Step 1

Understand Customer Requirements

The first activity of the audit should be to define customer requirements. Care should be taken that these requirements be drawn directly from the customer. They should not be reflections of a company's own beliefs about what customers expect. In a study of over 450 North American suppliers and their customers, A.T. Kearney found a substantial gap between the understanding of suppliers and customers on key requirements in all but a third of the companies surveyed. Over 90 percent of the customers complained that suppliers misunderstand the impact of their actions on the customer's own quality and productivity efforts. Key results from this study are illustrated in Figure 10.

FIGURE 10
CUSTOMER'S VIEWS OF IMPEDIMENTS TO QUALITY SERVICE

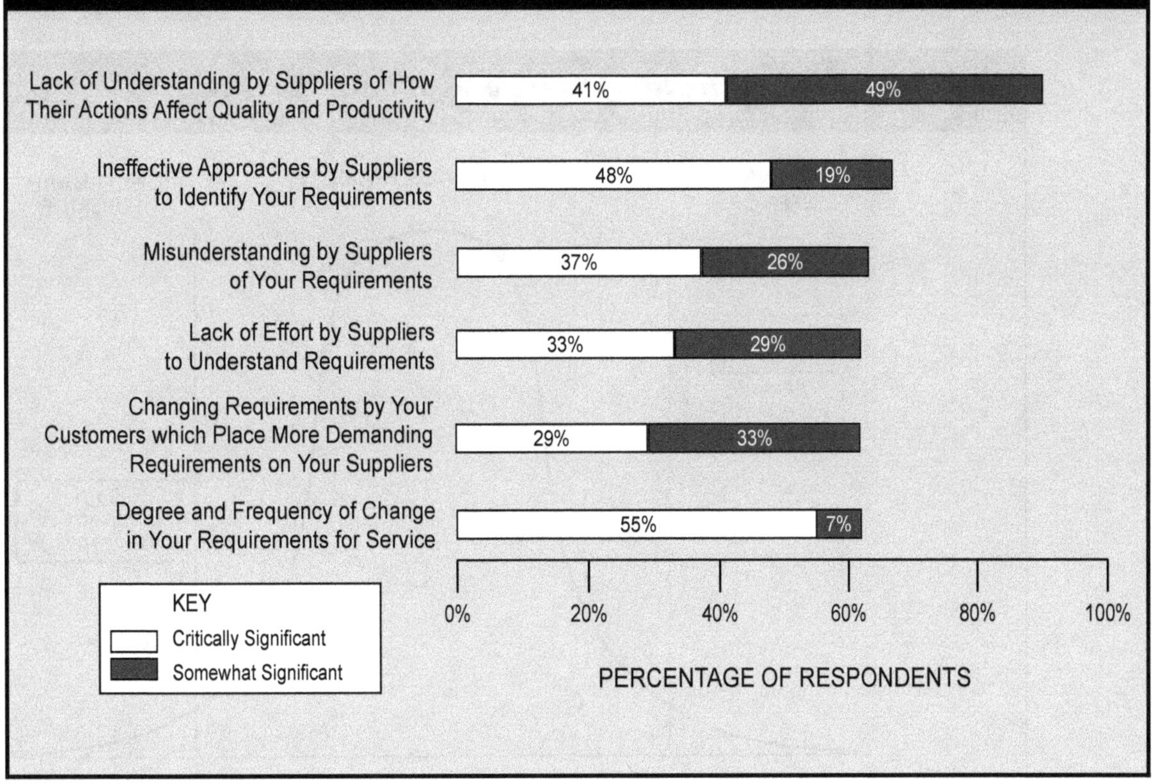

How to Know What Customers Want

When asked to define what they need from their suppliers, customers almost always seem to respond by saying, "more, quicker, cheaper." However, in truth, customer requirements are far more complex.

To determine customer requirements, audit team members should interview a number of customers. In general, interviews should continue as long as researchers are gleaning new insights from each interview. For highly concentrated customer bases where 15 or 20 customers make up the majority of a company's revenues, it makes sense to work with each one in order to thoroughly understand each customer's needs. Where revenues are less concentrated, suppliers should start with their own best description of their company's different kinds of customers. In most cases, even large companies are unlikely to have more than seven to ten different types of customers, although exceptions may result when regional and regulatory influences make the customer matrix more complicated. Interviews should be conducted with the people in a customer organization who make purchasing decisions. Most face-to-face interviews will last between an hour and an hour-and-a-half. The interviewer should let the customer describe (at first without structure or prompting) the key service attributes that would lead to incremental purchase increases, or that might cause purchases to decline. In initial interviews, the discussion should not focus on specific competitors. In some cases, managers from the supplier company may conduct the interviews. In other cases, outside support may be used for the interviews in order to get unbiased responses. When outside interviewers are used, the interviews can be "blind," or not identified with a specific supplier.

FIGURE 11
GAINING COMPETITIVE ADVANTAGE THROUGH SUPERIOR SERVICE

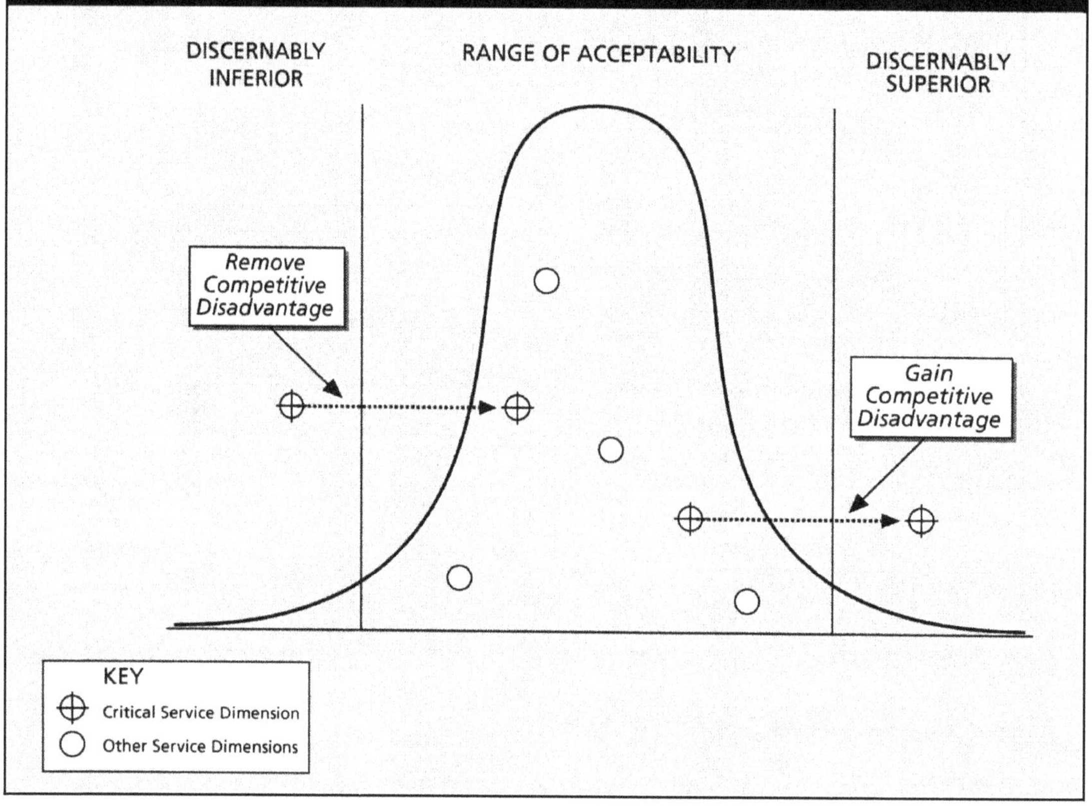

Interviews should continue until key responses are consistently repeated, and until unique responses describe exceptional or unusual customer requirements. This is likely to happen after about 12 to 15 interviews. Perceptions of customer satisfaction are subjective in nature, and superior performance is distinguishable in relatively few dimensions. Customers perceive the performance of most competitors to fall within a range of acceptability, as shown in Figure 11. Opportunities to gain competitive advantage rest on the development of a few fundamental capabilities that satisfy the ultimate consumer.

Interviewing Techniques

Using a blank sheet approach can help interviewers see through the eyes of the customer what is needed to improve satisfaction. If an interviewer asks customers about cycle time or fill rates, respondents will almost always say that they need to be respectively shorter and higher, even if that is not what induces them to buy more or less from a given supplier. By using a blank-sheet approach, an audit will get at the customer's priority requirements. A blank sheet approach involves asking respondents about what they value most in a supplier. This contrasts with a traditional approach of asking customers to rate a company's performance along any number of satisfaction dimensions. Using a blank sheet results in more valuable information because it relies on the customer's point of view, rather than imposing a list of the supplier's priorities.

In reality, customer requirements usually call for a complex classification system. Some typical categories identified as priorities by customers are listed in Figure 12.

FIGURE 12
TYPICAL CUSTOMER REQUIREMENTS

- Product line breadth and composition
- Order cycle consistency and reliability
- On-time delivery
- Order accuracy
- Product substitution
- Backorder policies
- Online order status information
- Order integrity (No split shipments)
- Product labeling and packaging
- Product receipt requirements
- Customer pick-up capabilities
- Shipment routing preferences and restrictions
- Minimum order restrictions
- Returns processing
- Telephone/online support
- Technical information support
- Market promotion information
- Damage rates
- Freight allowances
- Brand franchise and product quality
- Billing accuracy, and timing expectations
- Responsiveness to inquiries.

Understand the Customer's Unit of Measurement

The list of possible categories that can be identified by customers is virtually endless, and includes anything that customers look to a supplier to provide. To truly understand customer requirements, suppliers need to probe deeply. For example, when the customer talks about order completeness requirements, the supplier should know what measure the customer uses. Does the client measure by case- or line-fill rates, or by orders filled complete? Are there some items for which the customer expects 100 percent fulfillment, even though an average performance of 95 percent is satisfactory?

Regarding delivery promptness, it is important to know what "on-time" really means. Does it mean a time window, plus or minus two hours? Or does it mean delivery on a specific date? Or does it mean, "Just don't let my lines go down"? Are early deliveries acceptable, or are they as frowned upon as late deliveries? Is there a standard order, or is each order negotiated separately?

As important as what a customer requires in a commitment from suppliers may be the way in which that commitment is communicated. What role does the sales representative play? The customer service representative? Telemarketing? What about the role of the company's website and the range of different e-mail communications that customers receive?

FIGURE 13
CUSTOMERS' PERCEPTIONS OF SUPPLIERS' ABSOLUTE PERFORMANCE

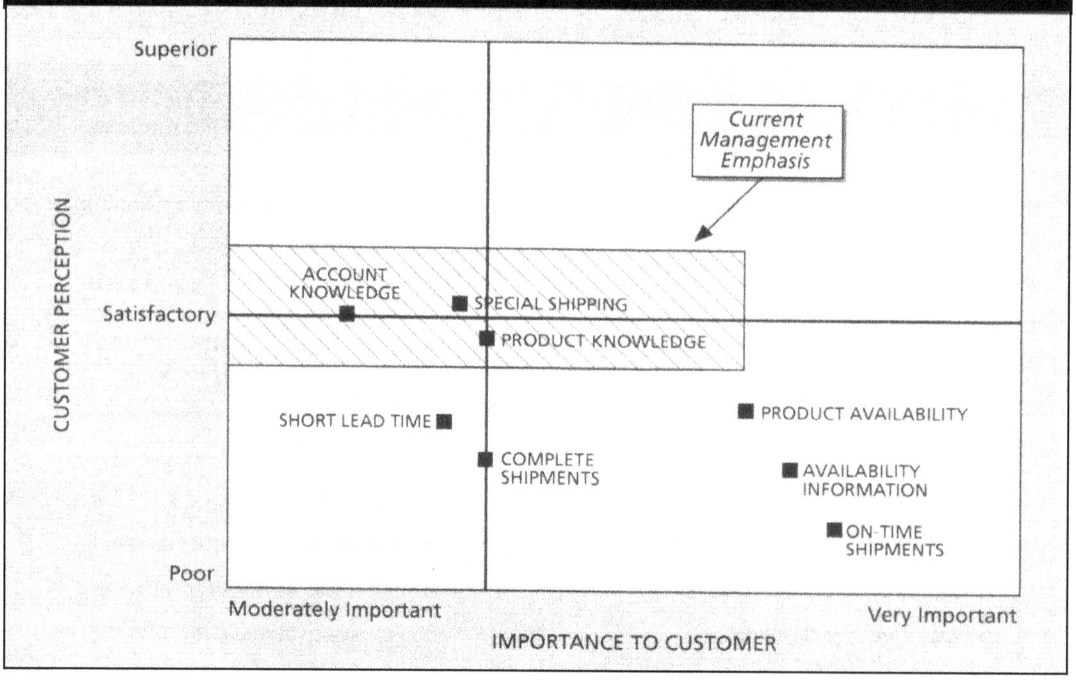

FIGURE 14
DEVELOPING AN UNDERSTANDING OF CUSTOMER REQUIREMENTS

SEGMENT XXXX		PERFORMANCE STANDARDS	
Customer Service Dimension	Relative Importance	Satisfactory	Discernibly Superior
On-time delivery	A	• 95% of shipments arrive on day requested	• 99% of shipments arrive on day requested
Repair service	B	• Response to service call in two hours	• Guaranteed recovery or loaner equipment in four hours

Map the Customer's Requirements

Successful companies map customer satisfaction requirements in a way that reflects not only the customer's perception of their service quality, but also the relative importance of the service attributes being evaluated. For example, Figure 13 shows the results of a series of customer interviews for a consumer non-durables company. It compares the importance a customer places on a requirement, as compared with the perception of the supplier's ability to meet that requirement:

By using this "customer report card" format, it is easy to see that the areas on which the company prided itself indeed met the expectations of the customers. However, it is equally clear that the customers did not perceive this service to be critical to their satisfaction, nor did performance in the more important areas of on-time shipments and availability of products and information meet their expectations.

Figure 14 shows a tabular presentation of this information. The detailed performance standards defining satisfactory and discernibly superior performance are particularly important for identifying opportunities to make a customer satisfaction breakthrough or set targets.

It should be recognized that customers often treat traditional measures of good service, such as fill rates and efficient order to delivery cycles as "givens." Customers' perceptions of a competitor's performance along these dimensions can undermine competitiveness. However, it is difficult for competitors to distinguish themselves, or create competitive advantage, by investing solely in these more traditional attributes of service. In general, these functions must be performed at parity with competitors in order for a company to satisfy its customers.

In addition to the interview data, audit teams should answer the following questions in order to more clearly understand their customers.

Customer Base

- How many active customers does the company bill?
- How many locations does it ship to?
- What is the concentration of customers billed (that is, what number of customers billed account for the top 50 percent of revenues; the next 30 percent of revenues; the last 20 percent of revenues)?
- What is the concentration of locations shipped to?
- How many key accounts have been identified?
- What constitutes a key account?
- What is the annual turnover of customers?

It is important to gather this information without considering internal company structures such as sales regions, territories, or accounting conventions that may obscure the true picture of the customer base.

Order and shipment profile information

- How many orders are received each year?
- How many shipments are made?
- What is the average size of order and shipment in dollars? [n line items?
- On average, what is the quantity per line item?
- Is there a minimum order size?
- Do these statistics vary by product line? By region? By customer segment?

This information can be structured in many ways. The key issue here is to make sure that the nature of the customers' business is seen as accurately as possible in terms of its stream of orders. The audit should produce an equally clear picture of how well the supplier is satisfying the customers' requirements through its stream of shipments. It is important to distinguish between these two pictures, and the operational implications of why any differences occur between them.

For example, a sporting goods manufacturer prided itself on filling every order promptly out of its distribution center. One of its customers was a large retailer with hundreds of stores. Each store generated three or four orders each week, which were automatically generated from their shelf management systems. Although orders were placed every night, receipts were only posted every Thursday. Imagine the surprise of the sporting goods company when the retailer expressed irritation that each order was being filled separately. Why couldn't the supplier hold the orders until Tuesday, and then ship one consolidated shipment to arrive just-in-time to update the inventory by Thursday night? The supplier had failed to recognize that neither the customers' order pattern nor their own shipment pattern accurately reflected customer satisfaction requirements. In this case, the supplier was able to both reduce the cost to serve and improve its customers' satisfaction levels.

Step 2

ANALYZE CURRENT CAPABILITIES

The second step in the audit process is to determine the company's current capabilities to meet and exceed customer expectations. The first part of this process is to clarify the company's current customer satisfaction strategy. While this strategy may not have been formally articulated, the following steps will lead to an understanding of how it has actually operated.

Clarifying the Current Strategy

Here is a sampling of some of the key issues that should be evaluated during this step of the audit:

- Are existing customer satisfaction strategies developed to serve different customer segments or categories on a differentiated basis?
- Is total customer satisfaction an integral part of the company's mission and strategy today?
- Are there strategic partnerships with key customers?
- What is the status of secure, electronic links with customers and other online communications based on common business processes?
- What special services are provided to customers? What are the criteria for offering such services?
- Is customer profitability measured? How?

In addition to these issues, the audit team should gather background information on programs or actions for improving customer satisfaction that are currently under way or that are planned for the near future.

This overview information provides the inputs required to assess the sophistication of existing customer satisfaction processes according to the characteristics outlined below.

Assessing Measures of Customer Satisfaction

Many audit teams find that the only figures regularly generated and monitored by their companies are measures of financial performance and cost controls.

These figures provide little insight into whether or not achieving customer-defined targets are being met, or even if the company's current processes are performing effectively.

The measures needed to assess performance will be different for each company. They often also differ for each customer or customer group. Therefore, the audit team should classify the various customer groups currently served by the company. Because no company can efficiently serve all customers, a fundamental issue in this process is determining which customers are most valuable to the company. One classification that identifies customers in terms of their profitability is the customer value framework described below.

Determining the Value of Various Customer Groups

Services and service levels should be segmented in much the same way that products are tailored for various customer groups. This means that companies should assess their customer requirements in terms of service in order to avoid providing services that may not be valued by some groups (thus driving costs up with no real benefit), while providing service levels too low for other groups. Successful companies may address the needs of their most profitable or "Platinum" customers by creating strategic alliances with them which merge quality and productivity processes in both companies into a seamless, single process. This not only increases profitability, but also increases the cost of moving to a new supplier for these customers. To do this, measures will have to be developed that assess the contribution to overall profitability of each customer or customer type.

For "Gold" customers, or those customers who are very profitable but not in the same category as the platinum customers, successful companies may choose not to create strategic alliances. However, they will certainly tailor their customer satisfaction services to meet the needs of this profitable segment. For "Silver" customers, successful suppliers provide differentiated packages of products and services. The profitability of these groups justifies focused strategic investments. Effective companies will consciously differentiate between gold and silver customers. Figure 15 presents a model for classifying customers according to their profitability, and shows the impact of each group on the supplier's bottom line.

Managers in many companies are surprised when they find that sales sometimes cost more money to fill than they bring in. This is possible in most companies because effective activity-based costing methods are not widely in place. Thus, the impact of paying more for sales than they yield in profits is not clear. Research shows that perhaps only two-thirds to three-quarters of a company's customer sales actually cover related fixed and variable costs. This is consistent with the widely-held conclusion that approximately 30 percent to 40 percent of a typical costs of goods sold figure is "non-value adding" or "costs of poor quality".

FIGURE 15
"EVERY CUSTOMER IS DIFFERENT"

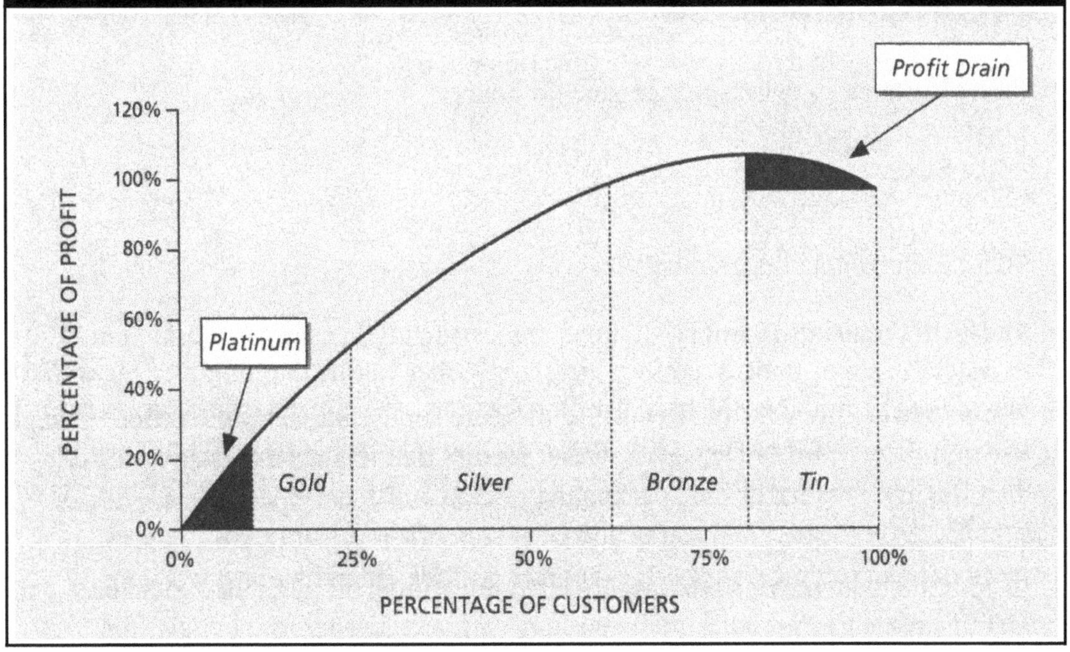

Customers who consistently make unprofitable purchases could be placed in the "bronze" or "tin" categories. Stage III companies manage profits on an account-focused, activity-based basis. Well-managed companies will avoid special services for bronze, or marginally profitable, customers unless they are specially compensated. Companies should find ways to make tin customers — unprofitable customers — profitable, or let them choose other suppliers. An important part of the audit process is identifying the bronze and tin customers.

Once customers have been classified according to their profitability, the audit team can explore what their company offers to the customers they value most. Then, the team should determine how their performance rates according to the demands of those customers. This can be done by referring to the data gathered in Step One, and determining how to measure the company's ability to meet the criteria outlined by customers.

Goals and Performance Measures

In addition to unique measures that are identified, the audit team should identify which of the following measurement processes are used in the company. For those that are in place, the team should determine what goals are being targeted and what actual performance is being achieved:

- Order completion rate (in percent)

• First pass line fill rate (in percent)

• First pass item fill rate (in percent)

• Order placement to delivery cycle time (in hours)

• Invoice accuracy rate (in percent)

• Shipment damage rate (in percent)

• Customer complaints (number)

The team should also identify attempts to measure total customer satisfaction through the use of indices or other measures. Other factors that might be measured include product quality, breadth of line, packaging; pricing and economics, terms, policies, profitability to customer; marketing and sales support, representative's quality, promotional and technical support; corporate policies, flexibility and working relationship.

In addition to identifying what is measured, measurement methods should be identified, such as periodic, online customer surveys, monitoring by sales reps, regular meetings with customers, competitive benchmarking, blind interviews or focus groups, etc.

This compendium of measurements and measurement techniques not only provides a foundation for mapping the current customer satisfaction process, but also will support assessment of performance against customer perceptions.

Most companies will know how much it costs to complete a shipment to a valued customer. However, few confirm that the shipment was delivered on time. In addition to considering the information provided in Step 1, audit team members should place themselves in the position of the customer and generate a list of all of the ways that satisfaction could be improved. It is likely that not more than one measure will have anything to do with measuring costs.

Step 3

Assess Competitors' Capabilities

Assessing competitors' capabilities is required not so much to define what satisfaction targets a company should set, but rather to identify any structural advantages or disadvantages competitors might have that allow them to invest in total customer satisfaction more productively. For example, a medical equipment manufacturer identified field service as a customer satisfaction requirement. One of the company's key competitors, which also happened to produce office copiers, used the immense field service force that supported the copier product line to improve coverage for their much smaller medical equipment product population. Duplicating this strategy made little sense for the company doing the research. However, an awareness of its use by a competitor led to the development of alternatives to compensate for the competitive advantage that resulted from it.

Identifying Competitors' Capabilities

During the process of defining customer requirements outlined in Step One, customers will provide a wealth of competitive information. This is especially true if customer interviews are "blind," with the sponsoring company not identified. This information is inevitably influenced by the process of collecting it, and is therefore not as objective as sources such as price lists, discount schedules, proprietary technology, etc. However, it provides rich data because it reveals the customer's subjective perceptions of the performance of various competitors. When these perceptions of relative performance are taken into account, opportunities to gain competitive advantage become more clear. Figures 16 and 17 show how this data can be combined with other measures to present a picture of customer demands:

Figure 16 shows the absolute customer ratings for the customer satisfaction performance of a manufacturer of medical diagnostic equipment. A review of these results would lead company managers to feel secure in their performance because the audit shows satisfactory ratings across the board, with some superior marks for their technical telephone support. When the customers' perceptions of best-in-class competitor performance is examined along those same attributes, however, the competitive challenges this company faces become more obvious. This comparison is diagrammed in Figure 17.

The X-axis in Figure 17 has remained the same as that in Figure 16, with a scale ranging from moderate importance to high importance. However, the Y-axis now shows a range from competitive disadvantage through competitive parity with best-in-class performance in that attribute, through to competitive advantage. This scale

FIGURE 16
CUSTOMER PERCEPTIONS — ABSOLUTE RATINGS

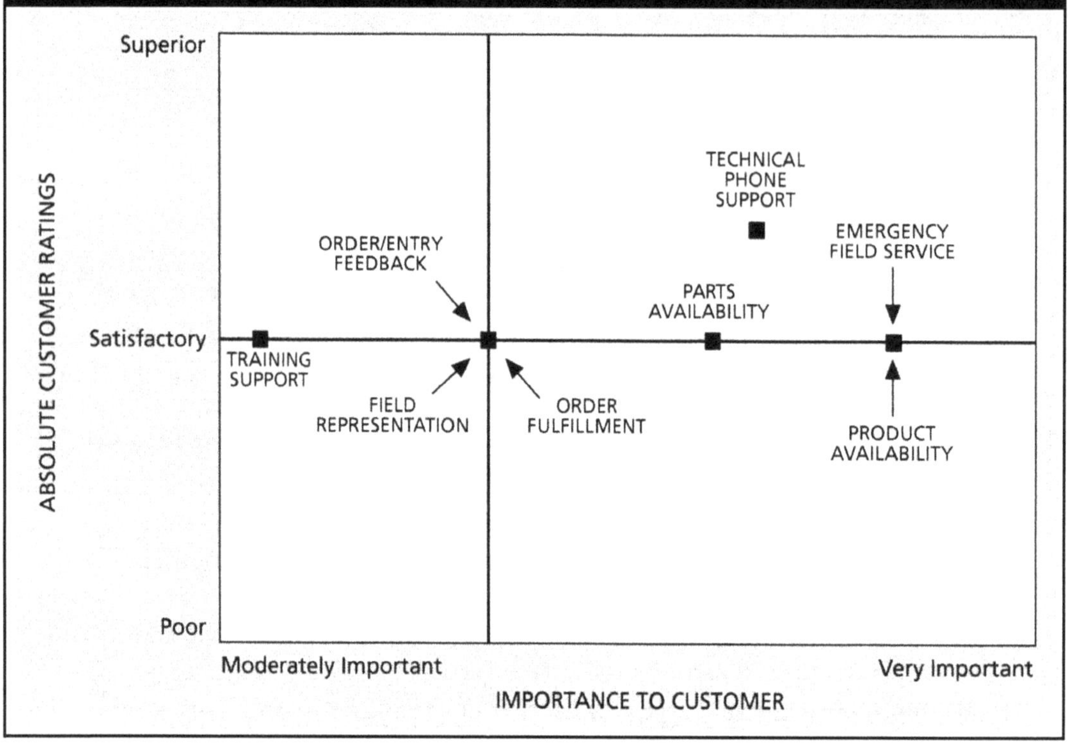

FIGURE 17
CUSTOMER PERCEPTIONS — RELATIVE TO BEST PRACTICES

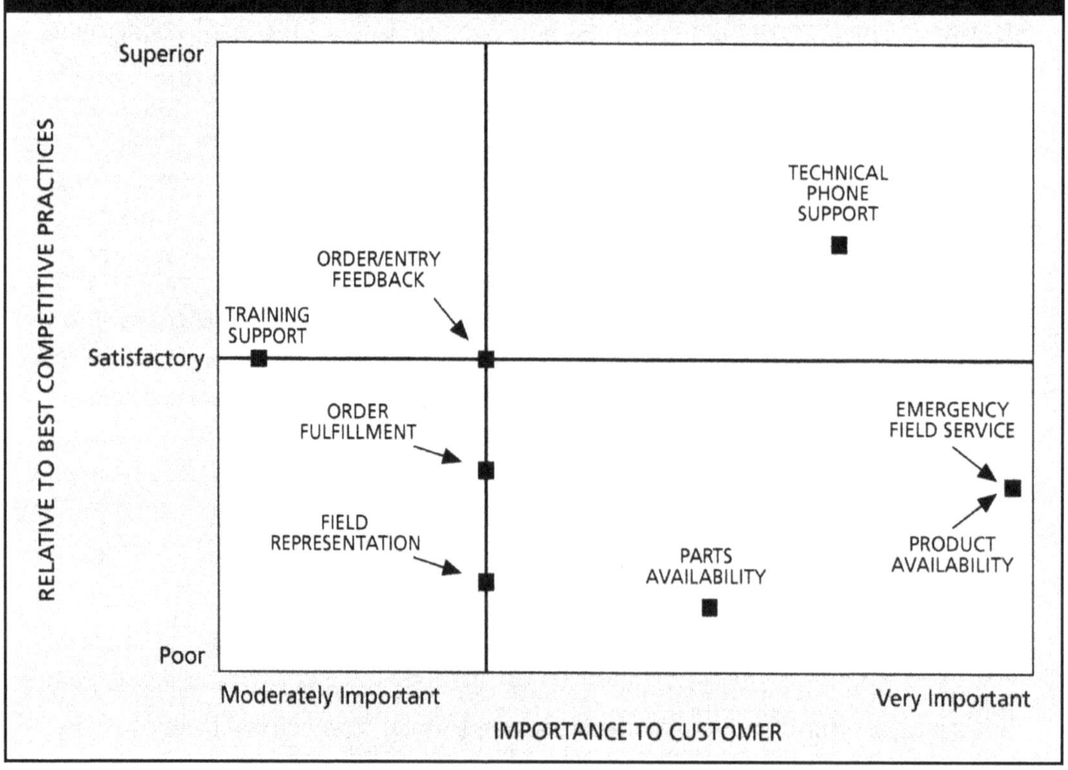

makes it apparent that the company in question faces competitive challenges in many areas: product and parts availability, field representation and emergency service, and order fulfillment.

Step 4

Identify Gaps

The purpose of this step is to identify gaps between what a company can reliably produce with its current capabilities and what customers have identified as their requirements for satisfaction.

Mapping the Customer Satisfaction Processes

In order to identify opportunities to achieve customer satisfaction breakthroughs, current processes must be mapped in a clear and revealing manner. Numerous tools exist to support the audit team in this effort. Process analysis tools, such as flow charts, cause-and-effect diagrams and group brainstorming techniques, help the team to understand how a process works. Critical questions to be answered at this phase of the audit include:

- What steps take place in each process?
- Where are decisions made?
- What are the key elements of the process that drive customer satisfaction?

Statistical analysis tools, such as time distributions, histograms, check sheets, pareto analysis, and control charts, help the team to describe the processes. The value of mapping current processes comes in understanding both the efficiency and outputs of key customer satisfaction processes. This aids the team in understanding the dynamics of the customer satisfaction process in question. There may be eight or ten parallel and interlocking processes, each of which has an impact on customer perceptions.

After the team has identified the processes, it should layout the actions, decisions and drivers in that process. The process map should be detailed enough to give someone not familiar with the process a good road map through the organization. The following method will result in the creation of a useful framework:

- In a meeting of the audit team, a large sheet of paper should be taped to one wall. Team members should use a large coin to trace a circle on the paper. Then they should identify a process action, decision, or driver, and write its name in the circle. For example, if the process is customer order fulfillment, then the first circle might read, "Receive customer orders".
- Team members should work to the left, identifying steps that precede receiving customer orders. This should be continued until they have reached the beginning

of the process. Steps in the order fulfillment process might include such things as the various ways that orders are sent in. A separate circle would be drawn for each of the ways of sending in orders (telephone, online, brokers, sales staff, etc.).

- The chart should then be extended to the right to show the steps in the order fulfillment process that come after customer orders are received. For example, a credit manager might decide whether to hold the order or fill it immediately. Separate circles should extend from this step in order to follow what happens under each set of conditions. This process should continue until the entire cycle has been mapped.

While numerous software packages exist to automate the recording of business processes, paper-based process mapping is still the most useful way for a team to work together at this stage.

Process-mapping is extremely effective in showing where a process can be improved. It will show weaknesses in the process, places where steps could be taken to meet customer demands, and areas where steps overlap or are duplicated. This will result in the elimination of gaps between customer expectations and a company's ability to satisfy those demands.

Step 5

Identify Options to Gain Strategic Service Advantage

To establish competitive advantage through customer satisfaction, options should be identified to increase satisfaction through specific improvement opportunities. This can be done by bringing together key people from all areas of the company to examine the data resulting from research in the early stages of the audit. Then, this group of leaders should explore options suggested by the data that make sense in terms of the company's culture, resources, and history.

This analysis should start by looking at what the company currently does well. This can be determined by asking and answering the following questions:

- What do customers see as being our strengths? What do they think are our weaknesses?
- What do we do better than our competitors? In what ways are we weaker?
- What changes would be required for us to develop core capabilities that are superior to those of our competitors?
- What type of customers do we serve? What type do we not serve?
- Of the requirements outlined by our customers and prospective customers in Step One of the audit, which ones match our current strengths and resources? Which ones do we lack the skills to adopt? For which ones could we easily acquire or learn the skills needed?
- Of the requirements outlined by our customers and prospective customers, which ones fit with our company's culture? Which ones are not well suited to our way of doing business?
- What are the demands of our gold and platinum customers? What resources and skills do we need to meet those demands?
- Given our company's current strengths and resources, are there customers that we could potentially satisfy who are not now being reached? What would it take to satisfy those customers?

Most often, options to gain strategic service advantage will come from changing the way things are being done today. Some of the areas where major changes might be required include the following:

- Product design
- Improved facilities or equipment
- Improved distribution networks that increase responsiveness and reliability
- Improved information systems
- Employee training geared toward increasing customer satisfaction

Improvement in any of these areas requires an investment of time and money. If the appropriate action is taken, it will lead to an increase in customer satisfaction. However, most companies lack the resources to improve all aspects of customer satisfaction. Therefore, choices must be made according to the strategy, priorities, and resources of the organization. The next section will explore ways of evaluating those trade-offs.

Step 6

ANALYZE TRADE-OFFS

Once the options to gain strategic service advantage have been identified, then the audit team should analyze each option in terms of its trade-offs, benefits, costs, and risks. From this analysis, the options can be ranked according to their value and viability for the company.

What Are the Requirements of a Customer Satisfaction Strategy?

Opportunities that have been identified as a result of mapping current customer satisfaction processes provide a wealth of ideas, each of which has a cost and an expected benefit, a certain likelihood of success and a related risk of failure. Many tools exist to organize and evaluate the trade-offs implicit in such an array of process improvement opportunities.

Improvements in customer satisfaction require the commitment of departments and functions throughout the company. Areas such as order entry, customer service, web support, help desks, sales, and inventory control must all be committed to the process of improving customer satisfaction. This requires an integration of effort generally found only in Stage III organizations.

Moreover, the adoption of a customer satisfaction strategy should not be taken lightly. In order to be effective, the strategy should be accepted, understood, and embraced by everyone in the company who is involved in customer satisfaction. Broad-based commitment is necessary because focus is impossible without it. If people within a company are pursuing different customer satisfaction objectives, then resources will not be used effectively, and customers will be confused at best and frustrated at worst.

The following questions can help an audit team assess the merits of each of the customer satisfaction strategies under consideration:

- Who within the company supports this strategy? Who does not support it?
- Which departments involved in customer satisfaction have worked well together in the past? Which have not worked well? What could be done to bridge the gaps between functions?
- What resources are available to disseminate information about the new customer satisfaction strategy? How much new training would each strategy require?
- Which strategies are most important to our most valuable customers?

- How much does our culture support integrative efforts between functions or departments? Which strategies require the most integration?

- Which of our competitors are pursuing similar strategies? What strengths or resources do we have that might enable us to out-perform them?

Each of the strategies under consideration should be evaluated in terms of its impact on the organization, as well as in terms of its impact on the company's most important customers. Members of the audit team, along with other company leaders, should evaluate each option in terms of its ability to increase customer satisfaction, as well as the company's ability to effectively adopt and integrate it.

Step 7

Select Service Dimensions

When two or three items have been selected as viable options, the leaders of the company should work together with the team to create mechanisms that will improve customer satisfaction. This strategy should include prioritization of initiatives, targeting results, apportioning resources and setting milestones for achievement of goals.

The Stages and Improvement Activities

The specific initiatives that grow out of a new or revised customer satisfaction strategy will depend on the company's maturity. Customer satisfaction performance is most effective in Stage III; however, companies that are in Stage I or Stage II may create problems for themselves by pursuing Stage III goals too soon. Therefore, this section of the guide suggests typical improvements initiated by companies at each of the stages of excellence.

FIGURE 18
STAGE I TO STAGE II IMPROVEMENTS

Implementing measures of on-time shipment and order fill rate performance.	Developing a systems capability to provide customer service measurement reports.
Improving automated, online order entry.	Implementing a customer complaint tracking system.
Designing or installing a new order processing system.	Developing a capability for making emergency deliveries.
Eliminating bottlenecks and improving the ease of doing business.	Undertaking a cycle time reduction program focused on the order fulfillment processes.

Here are improvement actions that typically take place as a company solidifies its Stage II performance:

- Online confirmation of product/service availability.
- Continuous tracking of orders with capability to inquire on current status.
- Ability to acknowledge orders at time of entry.
- Service targets that are based on meeting functional goals 100 percent of the time.

The breakthrough between Stage II and Stage III performance includes many improvement actions that are based on the customer satisfaction process emphasized earlier in this audit. Some of these actions are listed in the table in Figure 19.

FIGURE 19
STAGE II TO STAGE III IMPROVEMENTS

Segmentation of customers by profitability or other dimensions.	Implementing measurements of total customer satisfaction, incorporating more dimensions than just order fulfillment service quality.
Instantaneous, verified, secure order transmission.	Management accountability and rewards based on total customer satisfaction performance.
Understanding customer requirements for value-added services.	Communication of customer satisfaction vision to employees and to customers.
Customer-driven forecasting and production planning.	Training and empowering employees to focus on customer satisfaction.
Online customer-specific inquiry capability.	Improving capability for special services..
Benchmarking competitor capabilities and performance.	
Setting differentiated customer service goals.	

Solidifying Stage III performance includes a number of improvement actions that use the process of continuous improvement in total customer satisfaction within the organization. They also extend the company's vision and commitment to suppliers, customer intermediaries, and other supply chain partners. A few of those actions are listed in the table in Figure 20.

FIGURE 20
STAGE III IMPROVEMENT ACTIONS

Customer satisfaction as an integral component of company mission and strategy.	Focusing on strategic investment in total customer satisfaction to improve competitive advantage.
Customer satisfaction integrated with total quality effort.	Proactive communication of order status to customers.
Formation of value-added partnerships with key customers.	Promised delivery date provided at time of order entry.
Process benchmarking and visits to customers.	Follow-up on complaints and problems to achieve win-win results.
Meeting with customers to review their perception of service quality and performance..	Joint efforts to reduce total systems inventories and cycle time.

Improvement actions that are planned or that have been implemented by a company should be evaluated against the list shown above to help determine the sophistication of its current customer satisfaction processes and to identify potential opportunities for further development.

Step 8

Structure Service Offerings and Set Goals

The customer satisfaction audit should become a regular part of the satisfaction management process. Customer satisfaction leaders repeat this process every 9 to 18 months. The following reasons highlight the importance of regular audits:

- The competitive environment is constantly changing. Frequent re-evaluation of customer needs and demands will ensure that a company's customer satisfaction strategy is on target and keeping pace with external changes.

- Once an initiative has been implemented as a result of an audit, its effectiveness should be monitored. Initiatives that fail to show the impact hoped for should be revised. Initiatives that address the problems they were designed to solve may be eliminated once their purpose has been served. Once improvements have been made, the audit process can point to new opportunities that will lead to further improvements in the customer satisfaction process. The audit is a systematic way of measuring progress and identifying new improvement opportunities.

- Enthusiasm for improving customer satisfaction will inevitably diminish after a few months. Conducting a new audit can increase motivation to improve customer satisfaction inasmuch as it can demonstrate progress and point to further needs. Thus, the audit can help managers maintain momentum for their customer satisfaction processes.

The On-Going Audit Team

When the audit is repeated, it may be wise to continue with some of the same team members in order to provide leadership and ensure continuity. However, the process of conducting an audit can be a valuable training tool to help others understand the customer satisfaction process and how it can be improved. Moreover, those who conduct the research are most likely to feel the need to implement changes in the system. Therefore, executives may find it helpful to rotate team members, with a few new members joining those who have participated in previous audits.

SUMMARY

This self-assessment has presented a method for auditing the focus on total customer satisfaction in three ways:

- Through a comprehensive discussion of the concepts underlying total customer satisfaction as a strategy for achieving and maintaining competitive advantage.
- By describing in detail the process used by leading companies to develop a strategy for totally satisfying customers.
- By providing diagnostic guides and checklists for assessing the sophistication of existing customer satisfaction processes.

Total customer satisfaction is a journey rather than a destination. Success requires a passionate conviction that the only sustainable competitive advantage is one that is based on totally satisfying customers. It requires an ability to identify opportunities for maximizing the use of resources and a willingness to redesign current business processes in order to take advantage of those opportunities. Competitive success implies partnerships with other companies in the same supply chain, and commitment to people within the company. Finally, success requires persistence in order to achieve results in the long term.

FIGURE 21
RECENT KEARNEY STUDIES OF BEST-PERFORMING COMPANIES

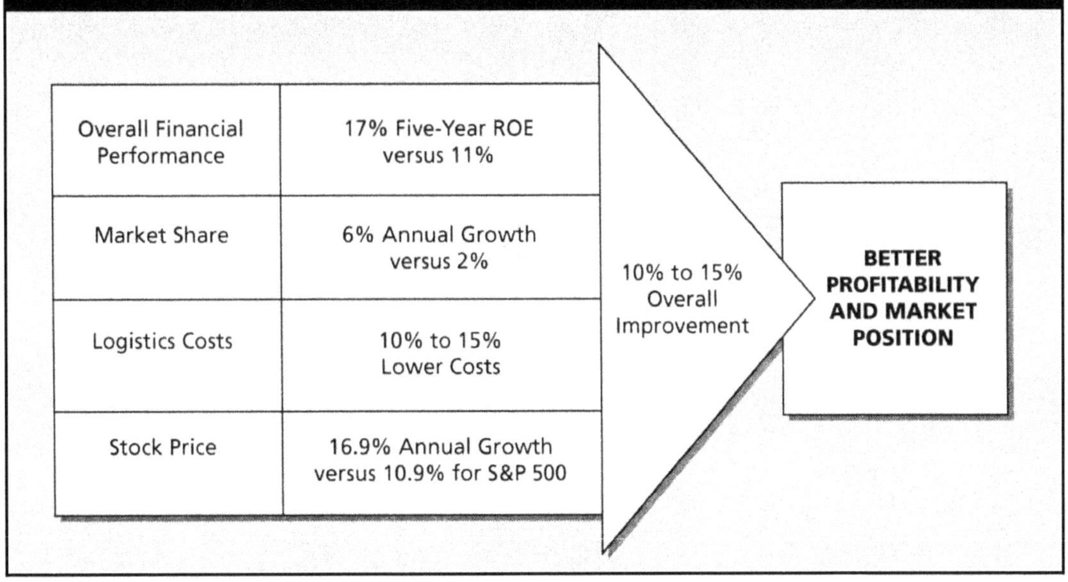

The results of long-term commitment to customer satisfaction are impressive. Customer-focused companies perform better than their counterparts with other priorities. As Figure 21 shows, the best-performing customer focused companies exceed the performance of their competitors along the following measures:

- Return on equity is six points higher.
- Market share growth rates are three times their industry averages.
- Operations costs are significantly reduced.
- Market capitalization growth rates are over 50 percent higher based on share price.

With results like these, perhaps it is accurate to say "Service with a smile" after all!

Part 2

The Audit Process

This section addresses the logistical and process requirements of conducting an audit. The topics covered in this section include:

- Staffing the audit team
- Creating an audit project plan
- Laying the groundwork for the audit
- Analyzing audit results
- Sharing audit results
- Writing effective audit reports
- Dealing with resistance to audit recommendations
- Building an ongoing audit program

STAFFING THE AUDIT TEAM

Who conducts the audit is as important in many ways as how the audit is conducted. In fact, the people selected for the audit team will, in large part, determine how the audit is done, how results are analyzed, and how findings are reported. The following list includes general characteristics of effective audit teams for most areas:

- Consists of three to four people.
- Reports to CEO or other senior executive.
- Represents a carefully selected range of skills and experience.

More than four people may be needed for an audit team if data gathering is labor intensive, as when large numbers of customers or employees must be interviewed. However, audit teams of more than six or seven people present problems of maintaining uniformity and communicating audit progress and findings during the course of the evaluation.

Selecting an Audit Team Leader

The audit team leader will play a strong role in shaping both the data gathering and the findings from the audit. The strength of the team leader will also influence the acceptance of the audit, both in terms of enlisting cooperation in the data gathering phase and in securing support for improvement initiatives that grow out of the audit. Because of the importance of this role, care should be taken in selecting the appropriate person for the job. The following qualities are found in successful audit team leaders:

- Has a good relationship with the CEO or with the executive-level sponsor of the audit.
- Is well-liked and well-respected at all levels of the organization, especially in the area to be audited.
- Has good interpersonal skills; can maintain good relationships even in difficult circumstances.
- Has good analytical skills; can assimilate and process large amounts of complex data quickly.

- Has some knowledge of the function or area being audited.
- Has extensive knowledge of the type of process being audited.
- Communicates ideas clearly and effectively.

Skills to be Represented on the Audit Team

Once the team leader has been chosen, audit team members should be selected on the basis of what each can bring to the project. Selection efforts should focus on developing a balanced representation of the following qualities:

- A variety of tenures in the organization, with relative newcomers preferably having experience in other organizations.
- A variety of familiarity with the area (function or site) being audited. Those who are intimately familiar with the area can serve as guides to the less familiar; those who are new to the area can provide objectivity and ask questions that might never be considered by those more involved in the area.
- Considerable familiarity with the type of process being audited. For this reason, many organizations call on people filling roles in similar processes from other parts of the company to work on audit teams.
- Good analytical skills.
- Good interpersonal skills.
- Good facilitation and interviewing skills.
- Good communication skills.
- An understanding of the company's strategy and direction.

CREATING AN AUDIT PROJECT PLAN

Creating an audit project plan accomplishes the following objectives:

- Ensures the allocation of adequate resources, or helps audit team members be prepared to improvise in the face of short resources.
- Ensures the audit is timed so resources are available that may be in high demand.
- Creates clear expectations in the minds of team members about what must be done, and when — especially important when they are not committed to the project full-time.
- Ensures accountability for what must be done, who is responsible for which tasks, and when the audit must be completed.

Financial audits often rely on the Critical Path Method (CPM) of project planning. This method was originally developed by the US Department of Defense to facilitate the timely completion of weapons development and production. It has since been modified to plan a wide variety of projects. The following outline is a simplification of CPM. It suggests the aspects of a project that should be taken into account during the planning phase.

Critical Path Method

In developing the project plan, audit team members should ask and answer the following questions:

- *What tasks must be performed?*

This list should include the major tasks outlined in the audits, along with sub tasks that grow out of those major headings. It should also include any tasks mandated by unique circumstances in the company performing the self-assessment. The audit team may want to brainstorm about tasks that need to be performed, then refine the list to reflect the work priorities of the audit.

- *In what order will the tasks be completed?*

Answering this question should include an analysis of which tasks and sub tasks are dependent on others. Which tasks cannot begin until another has been completed? Which tasks can be done at any time? The audit team may want to place the ordered task on a time line, with start dates, expected duration of the step, and end dates outlined for each task.

- *Who will perform each task?*

Most tasks will be performed by members of the audit team. These assignments should be made by taking the strengths of each team member into consideration, as well as the time availability of each person. Equity of work load should also be taken into account. If tasks are to be assigned to people not on the audit team, those individuals should be included or consulted at this point.

- *What resources will be needed for each step?*

Each task should be analyzed in terms of the personnel, budget, equipment, facilities, support services, and any other resources that will be needed for its completion. The team should assess the availability of all of the resources. Consideration should be given to the task ordering completed earlier. Are some resources subject to competing demands, and therefore difficult to secure at a particular time? How far in advance do arrangements for resources need to be made? Does the task order or time line need to be revised in light of what is known about resource availability?

- *Where is the slack time?*

Slack time is unscheduled time between dependent tasks. Slack provides a degree of flexibility in altering the start dates of subsequent tasks. Slack time signals that a task has a range of possible start dates. It is used to determine the critical path.

- *What is the critical path?*

The critical path in a project is the set of tasks that must be completed in a sequential, chronological order. If any task on the critical path is not completed, all subsequent tasks will be delayed. Delays at any point in the critical path will result in an equivalent delay in the completion of the total project.

Regardless of the method used to develop the project plan, no project, regardless how simple, is ever completed in exact accordance with its plan. However, having a project plan allows the team to gauge its progress, anticipate problems and determine where alternative approaches are needed.

LAYING THE GROUNDWORK FOR THE AUDIT

Once the team has been selected and a project plan developed, the audit leader should prepare those who will be involved in and affected by the audit for the team's visit or for data gathering. The following steps will help the audit to run more smoothly:

Communicate Executive Support for the Audit

Demonstrating executive support for the audit accomplishes two goals. First, it increases the chances that those involved in the area being audited will cooperate with data-gathering efforts. Second, it shows executive support for the area being audited and suggests a commitment to improving the area's performance.

In many companies, the audit is introduced by the executive sponsor of the audit by means of an intranet webcast or a more conventional written or multimedia presentation. The presentation should explain the purpose of the audit and ask for the support of everyone in the area being audited. It should be seen by everyone within the company who will be affected by or involved in the data gathering process. The most effective presentations explain how the audit results will be used, reassuring those who will be responding to audit team requests about the motives of the audit. Credibility is also bolstered when previous audits have been acted upon with positive results.

Make Arrangements with the Area to Be Audited

The audit team leader should check with the appropriate manager in charge of the process or site being audited to arrange for any required on-site visits, interviewing, surveys, focus groups, or written information needed for the audit. The team leader should also explain the purpose, scope, and expected duration of the audit; review the project plan with the manager; and answer any questions the manager has about the audit.

The team leader should also work with the appropriate manager or managers to determine how the audit can be conducted with the least impact on the flow of work. This may include discussions about the timing of the audit, the options for data gathering, the availability of needed data, and possibilities for generating the necessary information quickly and easily. Finding ways to make data collection more efficient and effective is especially important when the audit is part of an ongoing program, rather than an isolated assessment.

Develop a Protocol or Checklist

A protocol or checklist can be used by the audit team to outline the issues that are central to the audit. Written guides can help the leaders of those areas being audited to prepare for the audit. A protocol represents a plan of what the audit team will do to accomplish the objectives of the audit. It is an important tool of the audit, since it not only serves as the audit team's guide to collecting data, but also as a record of the audit procedures completed by the team. In many cases, audit teams may want to format the checklist in a way that allows them to enter their field notes directly on an electronic checklist.

The checklist should include no more than twenty major items, and checklists should be updated with each audit in order to ensure that the appropriate measures are taken. Items where improvement initiatives have been successful should be eliminated from the checklist, with newly identified possibilities for improvement opportunities added.

ANALYZING AUDIT RESULTS

Discovering gaps between a company's targets and its actual performance is a relatively easy task. Tools are provided to assist audit teams in assessing their performance in a given area. In most cases, more opportunities for improvement will be uncovered by an audit than can be addressed by the resources and energy available. Therefore, one of the most difficult aspects of analyzing the results of an audit lies in determining which opportunities are the most important for managers to pursue.

Because resources and energy for pursuing improvement initiatives are limited, choices must be made about which options are most important. Sometimes these decisions are based on political winds in the company, or on what has worked well in the past, or on personal preferences of top management. However, scarce resources will be used more effectively if allocated to the areas where they will have the greatest impact. Managers must also determine the most effective way to approach initiatives. This section discusses criteria for prioritizing opportunities that grow out of audit findings.

The Novations Strategic Alignment Model

For many years, the "excellence" movement, encouraged companies to achieve excellence in every area of endeavor. Although the movement created an awareness of the need for management improvements, it failed to consider that not all management processes are equal in terms of producing benefits. As a result, leading organizations in today's environment focus on performing well in a few core areas. Knowing what those core areas are depends on a clear vision of the company's strategy.

Strategic thinking about which areas should be improved involves much more than taking an inventory of current capabilities and weaknesses. If it did not, existing capabilities would always determine strategic objectives, and organizational growth and development would come to a halt. To set priorities strategically, companies must decide which improvement opportunities fall in the following categories:

- What to do themselves.
- What to do with someone else.
- What to contract others to do.
- What not to do.

FIGURE 1
CATEGORIES OF WORK

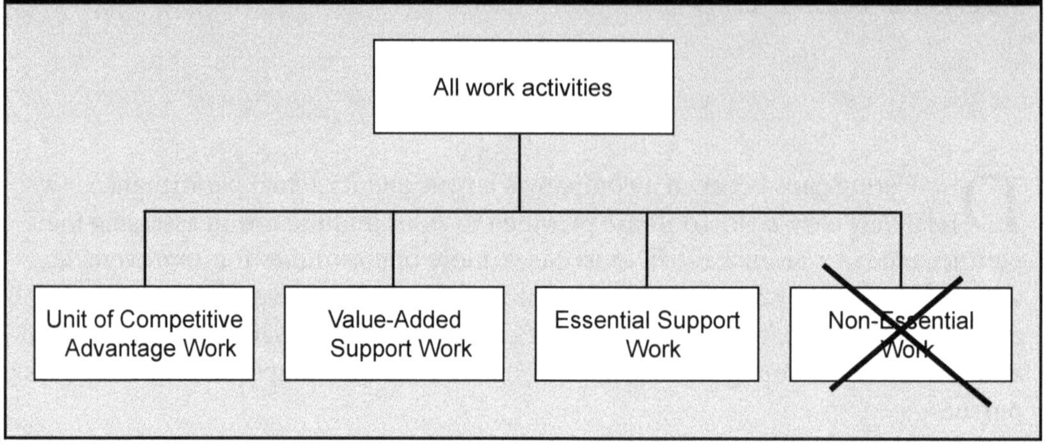

Figure 1 illustrates the four categories of work.

Unit of Competitive Advantage (UCA) Work includes work and capabilities that create distinctiveness for the business in the marketplace.

Value-added Support Work facilitates the accomplishment of the UCA work. For example, a company may have a technology orientation rather than a service orientation, but an effective logistics process may help them to improve their UCA work of providing cutting-edge technology.

Essential Support Work neither creates advantage nor facilitates the work that creates advantage, but must be done if businesses are to continue to operate (includes such things as paying taxes, maintaining payroll records, etc.).

Nonessential Work is activity that has lost its usefulness but continues to be done because of tradition.

Despite their sophistication in dealing with other aspects of business, most managers have archaic views of the different types of work. Many of their models for characterizing work have come from a finance or accounting orientation. Accounting terms such as overhead, direct labor, and indirect labor may be useful as a way to report costs, but they provide little understanding about the relative strategic importance of the work. Yet these classifications are frequently used to determine how work is organized and where resources are allocated.

The concept of *unit of competitive advantage* (UCA) helps to explain why some organizations either emphasize the wrong capabilities or de-emphasize the right capabilities. UCA also explains why some forms of improvement lead to competitive disadvantage, and why some businesses consistently outperform their competitors by gaining greater leverage from their competitive advantages.

A company's UCA includes the critical processes that create distinctiveness within an established strategic direction. It is based on the premise that businesses create competitive advantage when they focus their attention on a few key processes and implement those key processes in world-class fashion. For example, continuous improvement is a popular management program that assumes benefit from any kind of ongoing improvement. Generally speaking, however, continuous improvement programs will only create competitive advantage when an organization defines a strategic direction, clarifies strategic objectives, and determines its UCA. These crucial prerequisites tell where continuous improvement efforts should be focused to create maximum leverage. They suggest what kinds of work to improve interdependently, what kinds to improve separately, and what kinds not to waste time on. They even signal when continuous improvement is more likely to create competitive disadvantage rather than competitive advantage.

UCA Initiatives Should Take Priority

Understanding what work falls under which categories requires a clear understanding of the company's strategy. The initiatives resulting from an audit that affect the Unit of Competitive Advantage work processes should clearly have the highest priority among improvement projects. Value-added support initiatives should be second priority, and essential support work should be the third priority. Nonessential work should not be continued.

Once improvement opportunities that will have the greatest impact on the achievement of the company's goals have been identified, the following ideas can be used to lend further insight into how opportunities identified through an audit should be prioritized:

- *Focus on the two or three most important areas.*

Insisting that action be taken on all of the problems uncovered by the audit may overwhelm the people who are responsible for bringing about those changes. Flatter organizations and leaner work forces mean that people are already being asked to do more work with fewer resources and less time. Producing a long list of improvement initiatives may prompt people to dismiss all of them because they don't have time to complete the whole list.

- *Focus on the areas that can be changed.*

Emphasizing problems that are beyond the control of the people who are responsible to work on process improvement only leads to cynicism and a sense of powerlessness. By focusing on things that are within the sphere of influence, accountability for each part of the action plan can be clearly defined.

- *Include as priorities some improvements that can be made quickly.*

Rapid, visible improvement helps build support for more complicated initiatives. Quick improvements also reassure people of management's support for long-term improvement. Seeing immediate improvement helps to build commitment at all levels to the process, and helps build momentum for further change.

- *Emphasize the improvements that seem essential to long-term success.*

Essential improvements may involve sensitive issues or difficult problems, such as deficiencies in fundamental skill levels within the organization or basic strategy issues. These problems are not only difficult and expensive to address, but may also cause a great deal of personal pain or require significant individual adjustment. Nevertheless, long-term improvement requires a commitment to dealing with difficult issues rather than avoiding them.

SHARING AUDIT RESULTS

In most cases, audit results will be presented to various interested people in a feedback meeting before they are made available online. Those in attendance may include members of the executive team, managers who work in the area covered by the audit, the audit team members, and anyone else who is affected by or interested in the results. The meeting should be conducted by members of the audit team. The purpose is to present their findings, and make recommendations for capitalizing on opportunities for improvement.

Conducting Effective Feedback Meetings

The audit team's strategy for the meeting should be to present a clear and simple picture of the current situation as revealed by the audit. This may be a moment of truth for those who have been anticipating the audit results. The feedback meeting for an audit holds both excitement and anxiety: excitement that the future will be bright, and anxiety that shortcomings in individual performance will be highlighted and demands made for personal change. As a result, the meeting must be carefully managed in order to lead to productive change. The following structure is one recommended format for conducting a feedback meeting.

- *Introduce the meeting and preview its agenda.*

This might include an overview of the original intent of the audit, introduction of the audit team, and a brief summary of the meeting's agenda. This step should take no more than five minutes.

- *Present the audit findings.*

Audit findings should summarize the most important points revealed by the data gathered in the audit process. They should be presented separately from the audit recommendations in order to allow people to digest the two parts of the presentation separately. Clearing up misunderstandings about the findings may make the group more accepting of the team's recommendations.

The presentation of the audit findings should take comparatively little time. Audits almost always generate much more data than can be effectively presented or digested in a feedback meeting. The goal of the audit team should be to zero in on the two or three most important points learned from the audit, and present enough supporting data to illustrate those points.

Presenting too much data about audit findings has a number of negative effects. It encourages people to conduct their own analysis of the audit data. To a certain extent, this is a healthy and normal reaction. If others understand the evidence that supports the conclusions drawn by the audit team, they are more likely to accept and own the audit results. Therefore, they will be more committed to the changes brought about by the audit results. However, when people immerse themselves in large amounts of data, they may become victims of "analysis paralysis": they may spend unnecessary time attempting to explain contradictory data, or trying to understand methods used by others to gather data.

- *Present audit recommendations.*

Presenting the audit recommendations should be the central point of the meeting. The recommendations should grow out of the data highlights presented. The audit team should view the recommendations as discussion points for the meeting, rather than as absolute action items.

A common mistake in feedback meetings is to spend most of the meeting on presenting data and recommendations. It is easy for audit team members to become enamored of data they have invested considerable time and energy to collect and analyze. Others in the audience will probably also be interested in the details of the data collected. However, if too much time is spent on discussing the recommendations, the meeting will end before a commitment to action has been made.

- *Ask others to react to the data.*

The reactions of top management and those responsible for implementing audit recommendations will determine the ultimate value of the audit data. Therefore, the feedback meeting is a good time to resolve questions or problems with the findings and recommendations as they have been presented. If resistance to the audit findings is not resolved in the feedback meeting, opportunities for improvement may be lost.

Those attending the meeting may offer their opinions willingly. If not, the audit team members should ask the others in the room for their reaction to what has been presented.

- *Develop preliminary action plans.*

The detailed action plans should grow out of the recommendations made by the audit team. They should specifically address the question of who should do what by when. Formal accountability mechanisms should be established before the end of the meeting, such as the scheduling of subsequent meetings or follow-up check points.

Sharing reports more widely

The same rules that apply to the critical feedback meeting apply to the sharing of audit results across the organization.

While it is important to make the key data, principle conclusions and preliminary action plans quickly and available online, it is distracting and unhelpful to provide or circulate too much data. Once again, staff are likely to be distracted by the possibility of over-analyzing the data or engaging in protracted discussion of alternative interpretations when they don't fully understand the nature if the process being audited.

Of course, it is also important that the staff involved in the departments and processes that have been audited should not feel blamed for systematic problems or weaknesses. On the contrary, the most effective presentation of audit results will clearly highlight improvements that can result from the audit and generate enthusiasm for the audit process in other areas of the organization. The next section contains further information on this topic.

PREPARING EFFECTIVE AUDIT REPORTS

There are three fundamental purposes for preparing a formal report at the conclusion of an audit:

- An audit report may be a stand-alone summary of the audit. This approach is not recommended, inasmuch as the report is likely to be filed away, making the probability of action unlikely.

- The report may supplement a feedback meeting, providing those in attendance with documentation and an outline to follow.

- The report should also serve as a baseline document to make measurement of performance improvement possible in future audits.

Because the written report is the most enduring part of the audit presentation, it should be well written and easy to understand. The following tips will lead to the preparation of effective written audit reports.

Focus on a Few Key Points

The audit presentation should focus on the two or three most important findings. It is impossible to present all of the data gathered in the audit to those who were not on the audit team. It is also not advisable to present every detail of the data. The audit team members should trust their own judgment about what the highlights of the study were, and present enough data to support that judgment. For each of the major findings, the team may want to include the following information:

- What is the problem?

- Why does it exist?

- What happens if the problem is not fixed:
  - in the short term?
  - in the long term?

- Recommend solutions.

- Outline expected benefits.

Prepare an Outline Before Preparing the First Draft

A good outline ensures that the logic of the report is clear, and that ideas proceed in an order that makes sense. The following outline provides one approach that works effectively.

Background

This section should establish the framework for the audit in terms of:

- Providing a brief discussion of the overall purpose of the audit.
- Identifying the role of the audit team in the overall process.
- Establishing the limitations of the audit methodology to ensure that others utilize the results provided in the report appropriately.

Objectives

This section should identify specific objectives of the audit in terms of types of information the team was expected to generate.

Methodology

The methodology section should describe the mechanics of the audit and include the following information:

- Types of assessment used (survey, interviews, focus groups, etc.).
- Data sources, or the sample groups for each of the types of assessment used.
- Time frame during which the audit was conducted.
- Other pertinent details about how the audit was conducted.

Findings

This section is designed to provide others with a review of the "facts" that came out of the audit. Except in cases where an audit checks regulatory compliance, only the most significant findings should be discussed in any detail in the report. This section should also include briefly presented data supporting the findings.

Conclusions

This section should report the audit team's interpretation of what the facts of the audit mean in light of the objectives stated at the outset of the audit.

Recommendations

This section includes suggestions from the audit team on how to close the performance gaps identified in the audit. The degree of specificity to be included in the audit report will vary from company to company and audit to audit.

Appendix

This portion of the formal report should include any of the following items that are relevant to the audit:

- A copy of any questionnaires or survey instruments used in the audit.
- A summary of the data gathered in the course of the audit.
- Recommendations for subsequent audits based on the team's experience.

Present Audit Findings Accurately

Those who read the report will no doubt be somewhat familiar with the area covered by the audit. They may notice discrepancies between what they know about the subject and what is reported in the written document. Spotting one inaccuracy may lead the readers to discredit all of the findings, conclusions and recommendations. Audit team members should be careful to report data as it was actually generated, and to describe the impact of the findings accurately.

Use Clear, Concise Language

Every statement included in the report should be based on sound evidence developed or reviewed during the audit. Whatever is said must be supported or supportable. Speculation should be avoided. Generalities and vague reporting will only confuse and mislead those that the report should influence or inform. For example, a report using the terms *some*, *a few*, or *not all* can leave the reader confused about the significance of the finding. Specific quantities should be used, such as, "of the ten samples taken, two were found to be...", "Three of five respondents said that...", and so on. Statements should be qualified as needed, and any unconfirmed data or information should be identified as such.

Ideas that do not amplify the central theme should be eliminated. The report should not identify individuals or highlight the mistakes of individuals.

Use Good Grammar and Style

Basic rules should be followed in preparing the report. Below are some examples:

- Avoid extreme terms, such as alarming, deplorable, gross negligence, etc.
- Avoid using redundant or lengthy phrases, such as calling something an emergency situation when the word emergency alone will do.
- Avoid verbs camouflaged as nouns or adjectives. For example, use "the new procedure will reduce error entries," rather than "The new procedure will accomplish a reduction of error entries."
- Avoid indirect expressions where possible. For example, "Many instances of poor management were found" is more direct than saying, "There were many instances of poor judgment found".
- Use short, familiar words. Use words that are easily understandable to everyone and that convey the message concisely.
- Keep sentences short. Most writing experts suggest that an average sentence should be between 15 and 18 words. Packing too many ideas into a single sentence confuses and tires readers.

The audit team should provide enough background information in the report so that the reader clearly understands who conducted the audit and what the audit did or did not include. The purpose of the report as well as the purpose and scope of the audit should also be described in a manner that enables the reader to know why the report was written and who should take corrective action.

Timing of the Report

The timing of audit reports is critical to the overall reporting process and must be carefully thought out. In many cases, a written draft of the audit report is prepared one to three weeks before the feedback meeting. This draft then goes through a review and another report is prepared in time for the team's presentation. A final report may be completed after the feedback session has been held in order to record changes resulting from that meeting.

Presentation of the Report

The audit report will probably be made available on the company intranet to all interested employees, often with a short summary linking to more detailed conclusions and relevant audit data.

However, just as the audit program will normally have been introduced by means of a webcast or similar online presentation, so it will be useful for the same individual to make a brief presentation of the audit's conclusions. This will provide a measure of continuity and ensure that the audit team has the chance to emphasize the benefits of the audit to the business as a whole and to reassure those staff who may have lingering concerns that the audit is a veiled attempt to justify cut-backs or job-losses. A live question and answer session will also be useful if team members sense significant levels of concern or resistance amongst staff (see the next section)

Presented thoughtfully, the audit results can help to underline the company's commitment to its strategic objectives and help to generate increased commitment and participation at all levels of the organization.

DEALING WITH RESISTANCE TO RECOMMENDATIONS

Most audit teams feel that if they can present their ideas clearly and logically, and have the best interests of the company or department at heart, managers will accept the recommendations made as part of the audit and follow the team's recommendations. Many people who have worked in organizations, however, find that no matter how reasonably recommendations are presented, they are all too often not implemented.

Implementation usually fails because it requires people to change their ways of working. That change requires a great deal of effort, energy, and risk; therefore, change is usually resisted. Resistance is an emotional process; people may embrace recommendations based on their logic, but fail to implement them because of the emotional resistance to the personal change involved. Resistance is a predictable, natural, and necessary part of the learning process. Although resistance may cause audit team members to feel they have missed the mark in terms of the recommendations they have made, it actually often signals accuracy in having interpreted the organization's needs. By dealing with the resistance directly, audit teams can work through barriers to implementing process improvements.

What Are the Signs of Resistance?

In many cases, resistance may be expressed directly. Direct objections to recommendations are relatively easy to address, inasmuch as they can be discussed and resolved. When recommendations are being presented in the initial meeting, team members should stop frequently to allow those who are listening to the report to voice any objections or disagreements. Those who are presenting the data should be careful not to become defensive or to punish those who express reservations about the recommendations. It is impossible to deal with objections unless they are voiced; therefore, the audit team should welcome the expression of objections or differences of opinion. The following tips may be used for surfacing and dealing with direct resistance:

- Provide many opportunities for others to express their concerns.
- Carefully clarify any confusing concerns.
- Deal with important or easy concerns immediately. Defer the remainder.
- Summarize the concerns before moving on. Show that concerns have been heard.

If direct resistance continues, the following steps may be necessary:

- Talk about the differences of opinion.
- Voice concern and support for negotiating a resolution.
- Avoid struggles for control of the situation.

Dealing with Indirect Resistance

In other cases, resistance may be subtle and elusive. Indirect resistance is difficult to identify and deal with because its manifestations seem logical. People who are experiencing indirect resistance may feel that they are "getting the run around". Many different forms of resistance may manifest themselves at the first meeting or more widely across the company:

- Request for more detail.
- Providing too much detail in response to questions.
- Complaining that there isn't enough time to implement recommendations.
- Claiming that the recommendations are impractical.
- Attacking those who propose improvement initiatives.
- Acting confused.
- Responding with silence.
- Intellectualizing about the data.
- Moralizing that problems wouldn't exist if it weren't for "those people".
- Agreeing to implement recommendations with no intention of acting on them.
- Asking questions about methodology.
- Arguing that previous problems have resolved themselves.
- Focusing on solutions before findings are fully understood.

Almost any of these responses is legitimate in moderate amounts. For example, members of the group may have concerns about the audit's methodology that should be considered. Managers may realistically wonder where they will find the time to implement recommendations. However, if refusal to act on recommendations persists once legitimate concerns have been addressed, then the audit team is probably facing indirect resistance.

Many models used in sales training provide recommendations for overcoming resistance. These methods suggest the use of data and logical arguments to win the point and convince the other person to buy whatever is being sold. These models work well for direct resistance. However, indirect resistance is normally based on feelings rather than logic. Therefore, the only way to truly overcome resistance is to deal with the emotional processes that cause it to happen in the first place. It is almost impossible to talk people out of the way they feel.

Feelings pass and change when they are expressed directly. A key skill for audit teams that are attempting to implement recommendations is to ask the people who are presenting resistance to put directly into words what they are experiencing. The most effective way to make this happen is for the audit team members to address directly what is happening in the situation. The following keys provide help in surfacing and dealing with indirect resistance.

- *Work once or twice with the person's concern, even when it feels as if be or she is resisting recommendations.*

By attempting to work with the problem stated by the person raising a concern, audit team members can determine whether the concern is legitimate or whether it is an excuse for not taking action. If the issues raised are legitimate, the person should show some willingness to discuss and resolve them. If the issues are manifestations of indirect resistance, the person will probably respond with other forms of resistance.

- *Identify the form the resistance is taking.*

Paying attention to the dynamics of a discussion can provide important clues as to whether or not a person is resisting recommendations. If a person is consistently distancing him or herself from those who are presenting the audit findings, using gestures or postures that suggest tension or discomfort, while at the same time presenting arguments for why the recommendations presented are inappropriate, it is probably a sign of resistance. The non-verbal responses of the presenters may also signal the onset of resistance. If presenters feel that they are suppressing negative feelings or becoming bored or irritated, it may be further evidence that the client is resisting.

Once presenters become aware of the resistance, the next step is to put it into words. This is best done by using neutral, everyday language. The skill is to describe the form of the resistance in a way that encourages the person to make a more direct statement of the reservation he or she is experiencing.

One general rule for stating what type of resistance is being manifested is to phrase the statement in common, non-threatening language. Statements should be made in the same tone and language that would be used to address a problem with a spouse or close friend. The statement should be made with as little evaluation as possible; it is the presenter's observation about what is happening in the situation.

A second general rule for surfacing indirect resistance involves not talking for a couple of moments after the presenter has stated what he or she has observed. There may be a temptation to elaborate on the observation, or to support it with evidence. However, continuing the statement will reduce the tension in the situation. Without tension, the person who is resisting feels no discomfort, and is unlikely to address the issue directly. Moreover, elaborating on the original statement may increase the other person's defensiveness and reduce the chances of solving the problem.

If stating the problem in direct, non-punishing terms fails to bring the resistance out into the open, there may be little more the audit team can do to overcome the indirect resistance. The best strategy in this case is to avoid resisting the resistance. Team members should support the person who is resisting and proceed with the implementation of recommendations to the extent possible.

BUILDING AN ONGOING AUDIT PROGRAM

As the pace of change increases, and as organization leaders become more and more committed to continuously improving their effectiveness and efficiency, audits of all types of processes will become more common. The most effective companies will establish programs of ongoing audits, whereby a number of goals can be accomplished:

- Performance improvements can be measured over time.
- Important changes in the company's environment can be systematically monitored.
- Managers can make a habit of change and improvement, rather than resisting it.
- Those areas that are of highest importance to the company can be routinely improved.
- Processes can be modified to be in alignment with changes in strategy or in the environment.

As with all management techniques, however, an enduring program of ongoing audits requires that audits become integrated into the overall management system. The following guidelines are keys to weaving audits into the fabric of day-to-day operations.

Establish Support for Ongoing Audits

While support for audits begins at the executive level, ownership for the audit process must be felt throughout the organization if an ongoing program is to be successful. The following actions will help to broaden support for the audit process, while ensuring greater benefit from the audit.

- *Share the results of the audit with everyone throughout the organization.*

By keeping others informed about the results of an audit, managers reassure those who participate in and are affected by the audit of the integrity of the process. Employees sometimes become suspicious of probing investigators; they may have doubts about how the information will be used, or whether the information will be used. By sharing audit results, managers make an implicit commitment to improving the processes that have been evaluated.

- *Act on the audit results.*

Questions will be raised about continuing audits if early assessments bear no fruits. Failing to act on performance gaps that are identified leads to cynicism and lack of trust among those who work with the problems daily. On the other hand, improving a process can create the momentum that comes from accomplishment. Committing resources and attention to the improvement opportunities revealed by an audit also shows management commitment to the improvement process.

- *Let others know when performance has improved.*

Communicating the positive results from an audit is one way of rewarding the people who contributed to that improvement. It also builds faith in the effectiveness of the audit process. Moreover, showing that performance has improved is another means of reassuring people of a commitment to the improvement process.

- *Reward people for their part in improvements.*

Increasing efficiency and effectiveness can often be a threatening experience for those who are involved in a work process. Improving the way resources are used often means eliminating the need for some of the people who have been involved in the process. Although flatter, leaner organizations often preclude the possibility of offering promotions, managers should nevertheless attempt to ensure that people who contribute to performance improvement find their own situations better rather than worse as a result.

Rewards for helping to close performance gaps may span a range from thanking people for their efforts to planning a group celebration to offering bonuses or pay increases for improvement. Rewards are especially meaningful when people are allowed to suggest what rewards they would like for their contribution. This may provide managers with new ideas for rewards that may be less costly to the organization than financial recognition.

- *Involve a wide variety of people in the audit process.*

People can be involved in the audit process in many ways. By involving people from a broad spectrum, more people learn about audit techniques and results, thus spreading commitment to the audit process throughout the organization. By involving many people in the data-gathering process, employees feel that action plans growing out of the audit were a result of their input. Excluding people from the data-gathering phase usually reduces the feeling of ownership for the results, thus making people feel as if initiatives are being imposed on them. By the same token, involving a broad range of people in the development of action plans expands ownership for the plans and allows for the generation of more ideas.

Part 3

IMPLEMENTING A CUSTOMER SATISFACTION AUDIT: QUESTIONS AND CHECKLISTS

This part of the *Customer Satisfaction Audit* comprises a series of questions based on the eight steps given in Part 1. These questions have been designed to help you plan and implement your audit in a straightforward and practical manner, covering all the relevant parts of the audit in the correct sequence.

Who should conduct the audit?

The most effective tool for auditing a company's performance in terms of customer satisfaction is a cross-functional team of talented people that has the strong support of top management. Team members should be chosen carefully; they should be the people who are expected to lead the company in the next decade.

EIGHT STEPS IN CONDUCTING A CUSTOMER SATISFACTION AUDIT

- Step 1 Understand Customer Requirements
- Step 2 Analyze Current Capabilities
- Step 3 Assess Competitors' Capabilities
- Step 4 Identify Gaps
- Step 5 Identify Options to Gain Strategic Service Advantage
- Step 6 Analyze Trade-Off
- Step 7 Select Service Dimensions
- Step 8 Structure Service Offerings and Set Goals

Note: Before you answer the questions that have been listed throughout this part of the audit, you may like to refer to earlier sections of text, which will give you comprehensive information on:

- what to expect from a customer satisfaction audit
- the total customer satisfaction process
- why companies don't satisfy their customers
- requirements of an effective customer service program
- using the Stages of Excellence framework.

Additionally, useful background information is given for each step before the questions themselves are listed.

Step 1

UNDERSTAND CUSTOMER REQUIREMENTS

BACKGROUND INFORMATION

The first activity of the audit should be to define customer requirements. This can be done by addressing the following issues.

1 How to know what customers want.

2 Interviewing techniques.

3 Understanding the customer's unit of measurement.

4 Mapping the customer's requirements.

The questions below relate to each of these issues in turn.

QUESTIONS

1. How to Know What Customers Want

- In order to determine customer requirements, will audit team members interview a number of customers?

- For highly concentrated customer bases, where 15 to 20 customers make up the majority of a company's revenues, will the audit team work with each customer in order to thoroughly understand each customer's needs?

- Where revenues are less concentrated, will suppliers start with their own best description of their company's different kinds of customers?

Note: In most cases, even large companies are unlikely to have more than seven to ten different types of customers, although exceptions may result when regional and regulatory influences make the customer matrix more complicated.

- Will interviews be conducted with the people in a customer organization who make purchasing decisions?

Note: Most face-to-face interviews will last between an hour and an hour-and-a-half.

- Will the interviewer let the customer describe (at first without structure or prompting) the key service attributes that would lead to incremental purchase increase, or that might cause purchases to decline?

Note: In initial interviews, the discussion should not focus on specific competitors.

- Will managers from the supplier company conduct the interviews?
- Or will outside support be used for the interviews in order to get unbiased responses?

Note: When outside interviewers are used, the interviews can be "blind," or not identified with a specific supplier.

- Will interviews continue until key responses are consistently repeated, and until unique responses describe exceptional or unusual customer requirements?

Note: This is likely to happen after about 12 to 15 interviews.

2. Interviewing Techniques

- Will the audit use a blank-sheet approach for interviews?

Note: A blank-sheet approach involves asking respondents about what they most value in a supplier. This contrasts with a traditional approach of asking customers to rate a company's performance along any number of satisfaction dimensions. In reality, customer requirements usually call for a complex classification system. Some typical categories identified as priorities by customers are listed in Figure 12 in Part 1.

3. Understanding the Customer's Unit of Measurement

- Will the supplier probe deeply in order to understand customer requirements?
- For example, when the customer talks about order completeness requirements, does the supplier know what measure the customer uses?
- Are there some items for which the customer expects 100 percent fulfillment, even though an average of 95 percent is satisfactory?
- Regarding delivery promptness, is it known what "on-time" really means?
    - ❑ Does it mean a time window, plus or minus two hours?
    - ❑ Or does it mean delivery on a specific date?
    - ❑ Or does it mean, "Just don't let my lines go down?"
- Are early deliveries acceptable?

- Or are they as frowned upon as late deliveries?
- Is there a standard order?
- Or is each order negotiated separately?

As important as what a customer requires in a commitment from the supplier may be the way in which that commitment is communicated, as demonstrated by the questions that follow.

- Is the role of the sales representative apparent?
- Is the role of the customer service representative apparent?
- Is the role of the telemarketing representative apparent?
- Is the role of the company's website and online ordering and communication arrangements apparent?

4. Mapping the Customer's Requirements

- Will the company map customer satisfaction requirements in a way that reflects not only the customer's perception of the service quality, but also the relative importance of the service attributes being evaluated?
- Will it be recognized that customers often treat traditional measures of good service such as fill rates and efficient order to delivery cycles as "givens"?

In addition to any interview data, audit teams should answer the following questions in order to more clearly understand their customers in terms of:

- customer base, and
- order and shipment profile information.

Customer Base

- How many active customers does the company bill?
- How many locations does it ship to?
- What is the concentration of customers billed?

Note: In other words, what number of customers billed account for the top 50 percent of revenues; the next 30 percent of revenues; the last 20 percent of revenues?

- What is the concentration of locations shipped to?
- How many key accounts have been identified?
- What constitutes a key account?
- What is the annual turnover of customers?

Note: It is important to gather this information without considering internal company structures such as sales regions, territories, or accounting conventions that may obscure the true picture of the customer base.

Order and Shipment Profile Information

- How many orders are received each year?
- How many shipments are made?
- What is the average size of order and shipment in dollars?
- What is the average size of order and shipment in line items?
- On average, what is the quantity per line item?
- Is there a minimum order size?
- Do these statistics vary by product line?
- Do these statistics vary by region?
- Do these statistics vary by customer segment?

This information can be structured in many ways. The key issue is to make sure that the nature of the customers' business is seen as accurately as possible in terms of its stream of orders. But the audit team also needs to ask itself the following question.

- Will the audit produce an equally clear picture of how well the supplier is satisfying the customers' requirements through its own shipments?

Note: It is important to distinguish between these two pictures, and the operational implications of why any differences occur between them.

The second step in the audit process is to determine the company's current capabilities to meet and exceed customer expectations. The questions below will help you to do this.

Step 2

Analyze Current Capabilities

BACKGROUND INFORMATION

There are four parts in the process of analyzing current capabilities.

1 Clarifying the current strategy.

2 Assessing measures of customer satisfaction.

3 Determining the value of various customer groups.

4 Goals and performance measures.

The questions below relate to each of these parts in turn.

QUESTIONS

1. Clarifying the Current Strategy

Below is a sampling of some of the key issues that should be evaluated during this step of the audit.

- Are existing customer satisfaction strategies developed to service different customer segments or categories on a differentiated basis?
- Is total customer satisfaction an integral part of the company's mission and strategy today?
- Are there strategic partnerships with key customers?
- What is the status of secure, electronic links with customers and other online communications based on common business processes?
- What special services are provided to customers?
- What are the criteria for offering such services?
- Is customer profitability measured?
- How?

Note: In addition to these issues, the audit team should gather background information on programs or actions for improving customer satisfaction that are currently under way or that are planned for the near future.

This overview information provides the inputs required to assess the sophistication of existing customer satisfaction processes according to the characteristics outlined in the questions below.

2. Assessing Measures of Customer Satisfaction

- Has the audit team found that the only figures regularly generated and monitored by their companies are measures of financial performance and cost controls?

Note: These figures provide little insight into whether or not achieving customer-defined targets are being met, or even if the company's current processes are performing effectively.

- Should the audit team classify the various customer groups currently served by the company?

- Because no company can efficiently serve all customers, can it be determined which customers are most valuable to the company?

3. Determining the Value of Various Customer Groups

- Will services and service levels be segmented in much the same way that products are tailored for various customer groups?

- Does this mean that the company should assess their customer requirements in terms of service in order to avoid:

    - ❑ providing services that may not be valued by some groups

    - ❑ providing service levels too low for other groups?

- Might the company need to address the needs of their most profitable customers by creating strategic alliances with them which merge quality and productivity processes in both companies into a seamless, single process?

Note: This not only increases profitability, but also increases the cost of moving to a new supplier for these customers.

- To do this, will measures be developed that assess the contribution to overall profitability of each customer or customer type?

Note: These customer types and the measures that could be developed are given under the subhead "Determining the Value of Various Customer Groups" in Step 2 of Part 1. Additionally, Figure 15 presents a model for classifying customers according to their profitability, and shows the impact of each group of the supplier's bottom line.

- Once customers have been classified according to their profitability, will the audit team explore what the company offers to the customers they most value?
- Will the team then determine how the company's performance rates according to the demands of those customers?

Note: This can be done by referring to the data gathered in Step 1, and determining how to measure the company's ability to meet the criteria outlined by customers.

4. Goals and Performance Measures

- In addition to unique measures that are identified, will the audit team identify whether the following measurement processes are used in the company:
  - ❑ order completion rate (in percent)
  - ❑ first pass line fill rate (in percent)
  - ❑ first pass item fill rate (in percent)
  - ❑ order placement to delivery cycle time (in hours)
  - ❑ invoice accuracy rate (in percent)
  - ❑ shipment damage rate (in percent)
  - ❑ customer complaints (number)?
- For those that are in place, will the team determine what goals are being targeted and what actual performance is being achieved?
- Will the team identify attempts to measure total customer satisfaction through the use of indices or other measures?
- Do other factors that might be measured include:
  - ❑ product quality
  - ❑ breadth of line
  - ❑ packaging
  - ❑ pricing and economics
  - ❑ terms

- ❑ policies
- ❑ profitability to customer
- ❑ marketing and sales support
- ❑ representative's quality
- ❑ promotional and technical support
- ❑ corporate policies
- ❑ flexibility
- ❑ working relationship?

- In addition to identifying what is measured, will measurement methods be identified, such as:
  - ❑ periodic, online customer surveys
  - ❑ monitoring by sales reps
  - ❑ regular meetings with customers
  - ❑ competitive benchmarking
  - ❑ blind interviews or focus groups
  - ❑ others?

Note: This compendium of measurements and measurement techniques not only provides a foundation for mapping the current customer satisfaction process, but will also support assessment of performance against customer perceptions.

- In addition to considering the information provided in Step 1, will audit team members place themselves in the position of the customer and generate a list of all of the ways that satisfaction could be improved?

Note: It is likely that not more than one measure will have anything to do with measuring costs.

The next step in this audit is to assess competitors' capabilities. The questions below, which relate to Step 3, will help you to do this.

Step 3

ASSESS COMPETITORS' CAPABILITIES

BACKGROUND INFORMATION

Assessing competitors' capabilities will identify any structural advantages or disadvantages competitors might have that allow them to invest in total customer satisfaction more productively.

The questions below will help you to ascertain some of this information.

QUESTIONS

- During the process of defining customer requirements outlined in Step 1, have customers provided a wealth of competitive information?

- Does this information reveal the customer's subjective perceptions of the performance of various competitors?

- When these perceptions of relative performance are taken into account, do opportunities to gain competitive advantage become more clear?

Note: See Figures 16 and 17, which show how this data can be combined with other measures to present a picture of customer demands.

- Does the company face competitive challenges in areas such as:
  - ❑ products and parts availability
  - ❑ field representation and emergency service
  - ❑ order fulfillment
  - ❑ other applicable areas?

Having set out some guidelines for assessing competitors' capabilities, the next step is to identify gaps between what a company can reliably produce with its current capabilities and what customers have identified as their requirements for satisfaction. The questions that follow, which relate to Step 4, should help you to do this.

Step 4

IDENTIFY GAPS

BACKGROUND INFORMATION

In order to identify opportunities to achieve customer satisfaction breakthroughs, current processes must be mapped in a clear and revealing manner.

The questions that follow are designed to assist in this task.

QUESTIONS

Critical questions to be answered at this phase of the audit include the three below.

- What steps take place in each process?
- Where are decisions made?
- What are the key elements of the process that drive customer satisfaction?

Note: Statistical analysis tools, such as time distributions, histograms, check sheets, pareto analysis, and control charts, help the team to describe the processes.

- After the team has identified the processes, will it layout the actions, decisions and drivers in that process?
- Will the process map be detailed enough to give someone not familiar with the process a good road map through the organization?

Note: A method that will result in the creation of a useful framework is given in Step 4, Part 1.

- Will the process be effective in showing where a process can be improved?
- Will it show weaknesses in the process?
- Will it show places where steps could be taken to meet customer demands?
- Will it show areas where steps overlap or are duplicated?

The net result of this process will be the elimination of gaps between customer expectations and a company's ability to satisfy those demands. The next step in the audit process is to identify options to gain strategic service advantage. The questions that follow, which relate to Step 5, will help you to do this.

Step 5

Identify Options to Gain Strategic Service Advantage

BACKGROUND INFORMATION

To establish competitive advantage through customer satisfaction, options need to be identified to increase satisfaction through specific improvement opportunities.

The questions that follow will help you to identify these options.

QUESTIONS

- Will key people from all areas of the company be brought together to examine the data resulting from research in the early stages of the audit?
- Will this group of leaders explore options suggested by the data that make sense in terms of the company's:
  - ❑ culture
  - ❑ resources
  - ❑ history?

This analysis should start by looking at what the company currently does well. This can be determined by asking and answering the following questions.

- What do customers see as being our strengths?
- What do they think are our weaknesses?
- What do we do better than our competitors?
- In what ways are we weaker?
- What changes would be required for us to develop core capabilities that are superior to those of our competitors?
- What types of customers do we serve?
- What types do we not serve?
- Of the requirements outlined by our customers and prospective customers in Step 1 of the audit, which ones match our current strengths and resources?

- Which ones do we lack the skills to adopt?
- For which ones could we easily acquire or learn the skills needed?
- Of the requirements outlined by our customers and prospective customers, which ones fit with our company's culture?
- Which ones are not well suited to our way of doing business?
- What are the demands of our "gold" and "platinum" customers?
- What resources and skills do we need to meet those demands?
- Given our company's current strengths and resources, are there customers that we could potentially satisfy who are not now being reached?
- What would it take to satisfy those customers?

The next few questions explore how the options to gain strategic service advantage may come from changing the way things are done today.

- Will some of the areas where major changes might be required include:
  - ❑ product design
  - ❑ improved facilities or equipment
  - ❑ improved distribution networks that increase responsiveness and reliability
  - ❑ improved information systems
  - ❑ employee training geared toward increasing customer satisfaction?
- Will improvement in any of these areas require an investment of time and money?
- If the appropriate action is taken, will it lead to an increase in customer satisfaction?
- Does the company have/lack the resources to improve all aspects of customer satisfaction?
- Will choices be made according to the strategy, priorities, and resources of the organization?

The next section poses a series of questions, which relate to Step 6, that will help you to explore ways of evaluating those trade-offs.

Step 6

ANALYZE TRADE-OFFS

BACKGROUND INFORMATION

Once the options to gain strategic service advantage have been identified, then the audit team should analyze each option in terms of its:

- trade-offs
- benefits
- costs
- risks.

The questions below will help you to rank the options according to their value and viability for the company.

QUESTIONS

- Will improvements in customer satisfaction require the commitment of all departments and functions throughout the company?
- Are areas such as order entry, customer service, web support, help desks, sales, and inventory control all committed to the process of improving customer satisfaction?
- Has the customer satisfaction strategy been accepted, understood, and embraced by everyone in the company who is involved in customer satisfaction?

Note: Broad-based commitment is necessary because focus is impossible without it. If people within a company are pursuing different customer satisfaction objectives, then resources will not be used effectively, and customers will be confused at best and frustrated at worst.

The following questions can help an audit team assess the merits of each of the customer satisfaction strategies under consideration.

- Who within the company supports this strategy?
- Who does not support it?

- Which departments involved in customer satisfaction have worked well together in the past?
- Which have not worked well?
- What could be done to bridge the gaps between functions?
- What resources are available to disseminate information about the new customer satisfaction strategy?
- How much new training would each strategy require?
- Which strategies are most important to our most valuable customers?
- How much does our culture support integrative efforts between functions or departments?
- Which strategies require the most integration?
- Which of our competitors are pursuing similar strategies?
- What strengths or resources do we have that might enable us to out-perform them?

Note: Each of the strategies under consideration should be evaluated in terms of its impact on the organization, as well as in terms of its impact on the company's most important customers.

- Will members of the audit team, along with other company leaders, evaluate each option in terms of its ability to increase customer satisfaction, as well as the company's ability to effectively adopt and integrate it?

The penultimate step in this study is to select service dimensions. The questions that follow, which relate to Step 7, will help you to do this.

Step 7

SELECT SERVICE DIMENSIONS

BACKGROUND INFORMATION

When two or three items have been selected as viable options, the leaders of the company need to work together with the team to create mechanisms that will improve customer satisfaction.

The questions that follow will help everyone involved to do this.

QUESTIONS

- Will the strategy include:
  - ❑ prioritization of initiatives
  - ❑ targeting results
  - ❑ apportioning resources
  - ❑ setting milestones for the achievement of goals?

The specific initiatives that grow out of a new or revised customer satisfaction strategy will depend on the company's maturity. The set of questions that follows suggests typical improvements initiated by companies at each of the three Stages of Excellence.

Note: At this point, you may wish to refer to the Stages of Excellence framework, which is explored in detail earlier in this publication.

- Will Stage I to Stage II improvements come from:
  - ❑ implementing measures of on-time shipment and order fill rate performance
  - ❑ improving automated, online order entry
  - ❑ designing or installing a new order processing system
  - ❑ eliminating bottlenecks and improving the ease of doing business
  - ❑ developing a systems capability to provide customer service measurement reports
  - ❑ implementing a customer complaint tracking system
  - ❑ developing a capability for making emergency deliveries
  - ❑ undertaking a cycle time reduction program focused on the order fulfillment processes?

- Will improvement actions that typically take place as a company solidifies its Stage II performance come from:
  - ❑ online confirmation of product/service availability
  - ❑ continuous tracking of orders with capability to inquire on current status
  - ❑ ability to acknowledge orders at entry time
  - ❑ service targets that are based on meeting functional goals 100 percent of the time?
- Will Stage II to Stage III improvements come from:
  - ❑ segmentation of customers by profitability or other dimensions
  - ❑ instantaneous, verified and secure order transmission
  - ❑ understanding customer requirements for value-added services
  - ❑ customer-driven forecasting and production planning
  - ❑ online customer-specific enquiry capability
  - ❑ benchmarking competitor capabilities and performance
  - ❑ setting differentiated customer service goals
  - ❑ implementing measurements of total customer satisfaction, incorporating more dimensions than just order fulfillment service quality
  - ❑ management accountability and rewards based on total customer satisfaction performance
  - ❑ communication of customer satisfaction vision to employees and to customers
  - ❑ training and empowering employees to focus on customer satisfaction
  - ❑ improving capability for special services?
- Will Stage III improvement actions incorporate:
  - ❑ customer satisfaction as an integral component of company mission and strategy
  - ❑ customer satisfaction integrated with total quality effort
  - ❑ formation of value-added partnerships with key customers
  - ❑ process benchmarking visits to customers
  - ❑ meeting with customers to review their perception of service quality and performance
  - ❑ focusing on strategic investment in total customer satisfaction to improve competitive advantage
  - ❑ proactive communication of order status to customers

- ❑ promised delivery date provided at time of order entry
- ❑ follow-up on complaints and problems to achieve win-win results
- ❑ joint efforts to reduce total systems inventories and cycle time?

Note: Improvement actions that are planned or that have been implemented by a company should be evaluated against the list shown directly above to help determine the sophistication of its current customer satisfaction processes and to identify potential opportunities for further development.

Having completed Steps 1 to 7 of this audit, the final stage is to structure service offerings and set goals. The questions that follow, which relate to Step 8, will aid this process.

Step 8

STRUCTURE SERVICE OFFERINGS AND SET GOALS

BACKGROUND INFORMATION

The customer satisfaction audit should become a regular part of the satisfaction management process. Customer satisfaction leaders repeat this process every 9 to 18 months.

The "Questions" section below will highlight the importance of regular audits.

QUESTIONS

- Will frequent re-evaluation of customer needs and demands ensure that a company's customer satisfaction strategy is on target and keeping pace with external changes?

- Once an initiative has been implemented as a result of an audit, will its effectiveness be monitored?

- Will initiatives that fail to show the impact hoped for be revised?

- Will initiatives that address the problem they were designed to solve be eliminated once their purpose has been served?

- Once improvements have been made, will the audit process point to new opportunities that will lead to further improvements in the customer satisfaction process?

Note: The audit is a systematic way of measuring progress and identifying new improvement opportunities.

- Is enthusiasm for improving customer satisfaction likely to diminish after a few months?

- Will conducting a new audit increase motivation to improve customer satisfaction inasmuch as it can demonstrate progress and point to further needs?

- Thus, will the audit help managers maintain momentum for their customer satisfaction processes?

- When the audit is repeated, would it be wise to continue with some of the same team members in order to provide leadership and ensure continuity?

- Will the process of conducting an audit be a valuable training tool to help others understand the customer satisfaction process and how it can be improved?
- Will those who conduct the research be most likely to feel the need to implement changes in the system?
- Therefore, will executives find it helpful to rotate team members, with a few new members joining those who have participated in previous audits?

IN CONCLUSION...

All of the questions listed in this section will hopefully help you to plan an audit that will establish how to achieve total customer satisfaction. The extensive explanations in Part 1 will help you to answer these questions to best effect.

Good luck!

At the time of writing, **Michael Moriarty** is a principal of A. T. Kearney, Inc., a global management consulting firm based in Chicago. His consulting specialties include customer-focused logistics strategy, integrated operations management, competitive strategy and decision-making systems. Prior to joining Kearney, he was director of marketing in the International Group of Bell and Howell Co., Chicago. In addition to management positions in operations, logistics and new product development with Bell and Howell, he was site specialist for Book Inventory Systems, Ann Arbor, Michigan. **Abram I. Bluestein** is a vice-president of A. T. Kearney, Inc. He assists clients in improving their competitiveness through strategic and operational improvements. He has been head of the company's Global Benchmarking Center of Excellence, the Global Marketing Council and Centers of Excellence and the Business Marketing Strategy Group. **Ronald J. Sanderson** is a manager of A. T. Kearney, Inc. He is experienced in projects involving logistics strategy, business strategy, customer service, and marketing and sales. He has worked with the food and beverage, pharmaceutical, medical products and chemical industries.

ABOUT THE PUBLISHER

Business and Management Resources for forward-thinking organizations

Whatever name you give it, your organization is almost certainly looking for new ways to *outsmart competitors *win and keep customers *develop new products or services *train and motivate staff *cut costs and delays *increase profits.

Cambridge Strategy Publications has a highly-respected — and rapidly-growing — range of management resources to help you do exactly that. Now being used in more than 90 countries around the world, by organizations large and small and in every business sector, CSP's management resources will help you implement change fast in your organization.

- If you want to measure performance and implement appropriate change in any area of your business — look at our range of self-assessment audits. They cover all aspects of Marketing, Human Resources and Strategic Business Management.
  Visit www.cambridgestrategy.com or contact us at the address below.

- If you want to harness the power of High-Performance Teams, Total Quality, Benchmarking or Project-Based Reengineering — turn to our Portfolios in these areas. Each contains project guides and planners and a range of tools that you can put to work right away.
  Visit www.cambridgestrategy.com or contact us at the address below.

- If you want to share your experience of conducting this audit or get in touch with other organizations who have also used it— try our online audit network.
  Visit www.cambridgestrategy.com/networking or contact us at the address below.

Cambridge Strategy Publications Ltd.
Station Offices
Station Yard
Axminster
Devon. EX13 5PF.
United Kingdom

Tel: +44 (0)1297 631456
Fax: +44 (0)1297 631456
info@cambridgestrategy.com
www.cambridgestrategy.com

www.ingramcontent.com/pod-product-compliance
Lightning Source LLC
LaVergne TN
LVHW060213210926
848481LV00008B/2721